Zemke's Stalag

SMITHSONIAN INSTITUTION PRESS

WASHINGTON AND LONDON

The Final Days of World War II

Hubert Zemke as told to Roger A. Freeman

Zemke's Stalag

Copyright ©1991 by the Smithsonian Institution

Editor: Matthew Abbate
Designer: Alan Carter

Library of Congress
Cataloging-in-Publication Data
Zemke, Hub, 1914-
Zemke's Stalag : The Final Days of World War II,
as told to Roger A. Freeman.
p.   cm.
Includes index.
ISBN 1-56098-018-4 (hard)
1. Zemke, Hub, 1914-   . 2. World War, 1939-
1945—Prisoners and prisons, German. 3. World
War, 1939-1945—Personal narratives, American.
4. Stalag Luft I (Germany : Concentration camp)
5. United States. Army Air Forces—Biography.
6. Fighter pilots—United States—Biography.
7. Prisoners of war—Germany—Biography.
8. Prisoners of war—United States—Biography.
I. Freeman, Roger Anthony. II. Title.
D805.G3Z38 1991
940.54'7243—dc20   90-10042

∞ The paper in this publication meets the
minimum requirements of the American National
Standard for Permanence of Paper for Printed
Library Materials Z39.48-1984.

British Library Cataloguing-in-Publications Data
is available
Manufactured in the United States of America
97 96 95 94 93 92 91 90   5 4 3 2 1

Contents

Acknowledgments

Hubert Zemke's memory of the long-gone events in his action-packed military career during World War II is exceptional. Nevertheless, many records lodged in US and UK archives have been consulted in the effort to ensure accuracy, notably the National Archives in Washington and the Public Record Office in London. Additionally, a number of individuals who endured the deprivations of Stalag Luft I gave valuable information. They are: Roger W. Armstrong; R. J. Fayers; Royal D. Frey; George Hankey, OBE, LM; Wing Commander F. W. Hilton; James R. Martin; Group Captain N. W. D. Marwood-Elton; and Fred Rabo. Assistance was also obtained from Major General John W. Huston; Alex Vanags; Ian Mactaggart; Christopher Shores; and in particular, Patricia Keen. Bruce Robertson and Jean Freeman aided in preparation of the manuscript. Norman Ottaway produced the maps. If there were others whose help has been inadvertently overlooked, it is hoped they will accept apologies. To each and all the author tenders his sincere thanks.

Roger A. Freeman
March 1990

Introduction

Colonel Hubert Zemke, known as "The Hub," was without question one of the most colorful fighter pilot personalities of the Second World War. There is written evidence from those in the top echelons of the 8th Air Force that he was also considered their best fighter leader. This is not surprising in view of the combat success of the unit he commanded, the 56th Fighter Group, which led the field in besting the Luftwaffe and ultimately had a higher total of air victory credits than any other American fighter group flying in Europe.

The Hub's foremost attributes were an unremitting desire to succeed allied to an innovative and aggressive nature, the hallmark of every successful fighter pilot. He could be stubborn, irascible, and impetuous, aspects of character that did not endear him to many within his commands. Hub was never one to court popularity or suffer fools gladly. The job was paramount, and the desire to see his team the victors. His penchant for standing up to his superiors if he thought them lacking no doubt blighted his chances of promotion. The biggest black mark in this respect was accrued when he ignored a general's orders to remain in the United States and slipped back to his UK combat command. That Generals Spaatz and Kepner interceded with Washington in this episode and got him off the hook indicates how highly his prowess was valued in the 8th Air Force.

Hub joined the US Army Air Corps in 1937 and reached the cockpit of a fighter squadron a year later. In early 1941 he was selected to go to the United Kingdom to advise the Royal Air Force on the P-40 Toma-hawk fighters they were receiving from the United States. When Hitler attacked Russia, the RAF passed the remaining P-40s to the Soviets and Zemke was sent to help the Red Air Force master them. In this capacity he was probably the first USAAF pilot to fly with the Soviets during the Second World War. After a series of adventures he found his way back to the US and was handed the job of teaching Chinese to fly fighters. Then, given command of the first fighter group equipped with the large Repub-lic P-47 Thunderbolt, the 56th, he brought it to the UK and, after a checkered beginning, led it to its remarkable achievements. Not only was Zemke's Wolfpack, as the group was dubbed, the top scoring outfit, but it boasted many of the most famous fighter pilots, including the two highest-scoring US aces flying in Europe, Francis S. Gabreski and Robert S. Johnson. Hub, although disparaging his own capabilities, was an able fighter pilot himself, destroying or helping to destroy a score of enemy aircraft in air combat. His record of narrow escapes was also impressive; the fighter he flew sustained damage from enemy fire on no less than 12 occasions.

Ever one for a challenge, in August 1944 Hub Zemke forsook the most successful fighter group for the youngest and most inexperienced, the 479th. Into this he infused a similar magic, so that his new command also experienced a series of successes.

Eventually, the VIII Fighter Command, aware that its most successful fighter leader had run up a total of more than 450 combat flying hours, decided that he was long overdue for a rest. Grounding was the last thing Hub desired, and while he endeavored to persuade and evade, firm orders came in late October 1944 for him to report to the headquarters of the controlling fighter wing to take up a staff post. With his bags packed, he decided to lead one more mission. On this fate took a hand; in trying to escape the turbulence of a storm front, Hub's P-51 shed a wing and broke up. Instead of "flying a desk," The Hub was about to enter another phase of his wartime career, quite as extraordinary as that as fighter pilot and leader. The following narrative describes his adventures in Germany following his arrival there on the afternoon of 30 October 1944.

1

Prelude to Internment

My arrival in the land of my forefathers came with an almighty thump that winded me. All but the last few hundred feet of the parachute descent had been through turbulent storm cloud, with little time to see where the landing was going to be made until the impact. Fortunately this was in marshy ground, where icy water quickly stirred me into action. A short distance away were pines on higher ground and, picking myself up out of the mud, I made for these. The sudden breakup of the P-51 Mustang aircraft and blows to my right side as the seat parted from the fuselage structure had left me dazed and shocked. Shivering and with chattering teeth, I sat beneath the trees and tried to recover my composure.

The landing appeared to have been made in a marshy clearing in a pine forest. There was no sign of human habitation, giving good reason to believe that my arrival was unobserved. As the mind began to settle, thoughts of evading capture came to the fore. Struggling to my feet, I retrieved the parachute and, using an escape knife, cut a panel for a sling. My right arm was now so swollen and puffed that a fracture seemed likely. The rest of the parachute canopy and the G-suit, the inflatable anti-centrifugal force fitment, were hidden under bushes so that they might not be easily discovered by any passing German. The extent of the forest was unknown, but it seemed prudent to move further into the trees where it might be possible to light a fire and attempt to dry some clothing. Walking was painful, with my sore right leg beginning to swell; the right side of my face was swelling also. Darkness was falling, and faced with the prospect of having to spend a night in the forest I gathered some pine twigs and ignited them with a Zippo cigarette lighter. The sheltered dry material found directly under the low branches of pines was soon exhausted, and the larger branches fallen from trees tended to be too damp to do much more than smolder. The night was spent smoking Lucky Strikes and contemplating the future.

I estimated that the P-51 must have been somewhere southeast of Hanover when it went down, which would mean it was a good hundred miles to occupied territory where one might expect to contact sympathetic locals who could aid an escape. The compass in the escape pack could provide a heading, but the map included was not of a scale to be of any use in identifying my precise location. The prospect of a long walk would not have been that daunting but for the handicap of the swelling and smarting leg, arm, and face. Cold, wet, and aching, I had little sleep that night and at first light set off to the west. The sleet and rain of the previous evening had subsided, leaving wet undergrowth which soon soaked the clothing that had received some measure of drying by the fire.

The woods were soon interspersed with wide fields which had to be skirted cautiously, but until midafternoon the only signs of life were a few grazing cattle. Then, as the day was fading, I saw an old couple bent down cutting the tops from sugar beets with short knives and throwing the roots into a horse-drawn cart. My condition having become even more miserable, it was now obvious that without help there would be little hope of covering many miles. After considering the situation, I decided to approach the two farm workers. Being fluent in German—if a little rusty—I might possibly persuade them to help, particularly if they were disenchanted with the war and the Nazis. Or they could well be foreigners impressed into farm laboring. In either case it was probably naive to think they would dare to help a US airman, but this was a chance that had to be taken if my circumstances were to be improved.

So intent were the elderly couple on their labors that they did not look up until I had walked across the field to within speaking distance. Fear was immediately evident in their faces and the woman fled even before I had been able to utter a mentally rehearsed request for food and help. The old man pleaded that he was a Polish forced laborer and dare not help. It quickly became evident that there would be no assistance here and that the attempt would have to be aborted. As fast as my painful leg would allow, I made tracks for the woods, believing that the fleeing woman had probably alerted the neighborhood. This proved to be the case for, while attempting to cross a road from one piece of woodland to another, I was suddenly surprised by a group of armed villagers. Near exhaustion and unable to run, there was really no sane alternative to surrender. No attempt was made by my captors to search their prisoner as I was hustled along the road toward a house which appeared to be an inn. Here I occupied a kitchen chair while a man stood guard with a shotgun. The combination of shock and exposure were now having an effect and, when offered some soup, I felt too sick to accept. Although no one was allowed to come into the kitchen to see me, the continual hub-bub of voices from an adjoining public room indicated that my capture and presence were the cause of some excitement among the villagers.

Apart from the guard, I was left alone until late in the evening when two Luftwaffe officers arrived. They took me to the airfield at Celle where I was deposited in a lockup in the camp jail. At last I was able to remove my damp clothing, which was taken away for searching and eventually returned dry with the word "Kriegsgefangener" (prisoner of war) painted on the back of the flight jacket.

At Celle there was no attempt at interrogation, and after two days of incarceration I was brought before a Luftwaffe major and told I was being sent, under guard, to Auswertestelle-West, the interrogation center at Oberursel, not far from Frankfurt-am-Main. The consequences of trying to escape were made clear: a bullet. I was then turned over to two soldiers who appeared to be special military police assigned regularly to the collection and escort of Allied POWs. They both carried backpacks bulging with accoutrements which suggested they were frequently on the move. Departure from Celle was immediate, despite darkness having descended. We marched along a country road where one of the guards collected a girlfriend or wife. Eventually a rail station was reached and I was ushered into a waiting room. The chatter of conversation dropped away as the many German civilians present caught sight of the unshaven, black-eyed, swollen-faced American *Terrorflieger* in their midst. With my knowledge of German, I was aware of the hostile comments aimed in my direction.

The first train took us to Hanover, where a connection for Frankfurt-am-Main was to be made. During the long wait there was time to observe the traveling public of western Germany. From the large numbers present it was apparent that the danger of strafing aircraft in daylight had led most people to travel under the comparative safety of darkness. While there were many men in military uniforms, a large proportion of the travelers were women. Evidently rides in unheated carriages demanded a practical dress; women for the most part wore ski slacks or heavy skirt assemblies with knee-high boots, while men wore thick overcoats, mufflers, and heavy caps. People inquired about connections and directions from everyone. The station staff were continually confronted by a horde of bewildered travelers asking where to catch a train to this place or that, inquiring about the inevitable rerouting because of bombed tracks. It seemed that most everyone could strike up an amiable conversation with anyone standing or sitting nearby. Ironically, this casualness coexisted with sinister warning posters, plastered everywhere, depicting a shadowy cloak and dagger character having an ear the size of an elephant, listening to conversation. Also noticeable were a number of less well dressed men and, hearing them speak in other languages, I realized they were workers imported from occupied countries. It was surprising that they moved around so freely but I was to learn later that they were all volunteers attracted by big money.

After a two-hour wait the guards indicated that our train had arrived. As at the previous station, there was a rush to board, the throng of would-be passengers pushing and shoving to gain entry. The guards waited until the worst of this melee was over and then led their captive to a first-class compartment. The journey south took a day and a half, with long periods when the train was stationary, no doubt again due to the ravages of Allied air power. My guards were tolerably pleasant and shared their meals of black bread, blood sausage, and apples with me. I spent the journey reviewing the possibilities of escape, an enterprise that in my present battered state would be foolish to attempt; beside which the guards, while not hostile, were vigilant, one always remaining with me and alert.

Auswertestelle-West was finally reached with a trolley bus ride from Frankfurt station. While waiting outside an administration building for one of the guards to make arrangements to hand over their charge, I was joined by two other disheveled US airmen also under guard. Fearing they might be "plants," I avoided conversation. Since capture there had been no signs that I was being treated any differently from other Allied airmen, yet the enemy must have been aware they had an experienced commanding officer in their hands. Now I expected to be subjected to intense interrogation as the Luftwaffe must believe Zemke held valuable intelligence.

The introduction to Auswertestelle-West was an order to remove all my clothing, which was then minutely searched by camp staff. When back in my stained and crumpled flight suit, photographs were taken for identification purposes. I was next approached by a Luftwaffe lieutenant, who invited me into a room where a Red Cross form was produced. As, in my opinion, this required far more information than the name, rank, and serial number which were instilled as the only information to be given if captured, I refused to complete the form. The Luftwaffe officer became annoyed and called another interrogator of NCO rank, who used more forceful language. Failing to persuade their prisoner to answer the questions on the printed form, they had me escorted to another block and locked in a small room. The high windows had been boarded up and the accommodation was immediately identified as one of the solitary confinement blocks heard about in lectures on Luftwaffe interrogation techniques. There was no heating and a chill night was spent contemplating, between bouts of sleep, what was to come.

It was midmorning the following day before I was again taken to face my interrogators. Offering me coffee and cigarettes, the officer and NCO encountered previously again tried to persuade me there was nothing sinister about the form I had refused to complete. After a few minutes another NCO entered the room and greeted me with the suggestion that former members of my command, who were now POWs, would be pleased to see me. I pretended that the names mentioned meant nothing special, but it was quickly obvious that the newcomer had the most detailed and up-to-date knowledge of the personalities of the 8th Air Force fighter groups. This tall, lean, beaming individual had a most convincing manner, and I suspected that the man could easily charm an unwary prisoner into divulging the information required. Moreover, Gefreiter (Private First Class) Hanns Scharff, despite his lowly rank, was obviously the key interrogator of the establishment. Scharff asked no direct questions other than how I had been treated since capture. This was an opportunity for me to ask for a doctor's examination of my swollen and sore limbs, a request that had hitherto been ignored. Scharff commiserated and said medical treatment would be forthcoming. However, no doctor made an appearance and solitary incarceration continued for two days without further call for interrogation. All part of the mental softening-up process, as anticipated.

On the morning of my third day in solitary, I was taken from the cell building across to Scharff's office in one of the administrative buildings. As on the previous occasion, Scharff's manner was friendly, refreshments were offered and the guard dismissed. Again the interrogator's objective was to undermine the tight-lipped intentions of his prisoner with a display of facts about my commands and myself. I had endeavored to hide my ability to speak and understand German, but this supposed secret was now exposed. One of the first actions Scharff took on this occasion was to warn his secretary that the US colonel could understand all that was said. A large volume of cuttings and photographs covering former commands, the 56th and 479th Fighter Groups, was produced and topped with an extensive and accurate rundown on Zemke's service career. While I reasoned that most of this could have been gleaned legitimately from nonclassified official publications and US newspapers, it was evident that some of the material could only have been obtained from other captives whose caution had been undermined.

Eventually, as anticipated, Scharff attempted to elicit information on future strategy, of which a foremost fighter leader must be aware. I had already decided how to deal with such a development and explained that never having served at a headquarters, my contacts with generals were few and far between. As a combat commander I had never had any involvement in planning or associated matters. This to a large extent was true. Despite his inability to elicit anything of value, Scharff retained his friendly attitude to the end of the session, when his prisoner was again returned to his cell. Later that afternoon the cell door opened and Scharff and a lieutenant, named Hanemann, entered. If I would give a parole not to escape they would walk with me to a nearby hospital where a doctor would examine my arm. As the leg was much less painful there was no hesitation to take up the offer of relief from close confinement.

After a 15-minute walk along a narrow wooded road, the dispensary at Hohe-Mark, a former sanatorium run by nuns, came into view. It now served as the hospital to house POW airmen too ill or disabled to have normal Auswertestelle-West interrogations. The Luftwaffe doctor in charge was Hauptmann (Captain) Ernest Ittershagen, much respected for his dedication and badly overworked. Examining my arm and shoulder, he pronounced that there were no fractures but severe bruising which would take a few weeks to go away. The doctor asked how it had happened and, aware that Scharff was listening, I said I had been struck by something while descending in a parachute. The doctor suggested the swollen arm would benefit from a half hour under a sunlamp and instructed a patient swathed in burns bandages to assist in setting this up.

I discovered that the man was a captain I had once met at a gathering of fighter pilots in England. When the interrogators were out of earshot he gave some useful advice on interrogation proceedings. Before walking back to Auswertestelle-West I was invited to dine with the hospital staff and patients. It proved to be my first decent meal since arriving in Germany. A simple stew; it tasted like a dish set for a king.

Two further days of solitary followed, but the interlude at Hohe-Mark had considerably improved my morale. Then came a further invitation to accompany Scharff to the hospital. During the first visit it had been mentioned to the doctor that I had worked part-time in a hospital for a year while at university. Scharff said that the doctor had asked that I assist him in attending some severely injured patients. At least this was the reason given for my presence, and help was given in changing several dressings on some of the most horrific burns cases I had ever seen. Another task was to hold down a man while flak fragments were removed from his buttocks without anaesthetic. After this disturbing afternoon seeing so much suffering, I wondered if this was all part of the conditioning process for interrogation and what was to follow. Another two days of solitary followed and then, to my great surprise, I was informed that I was to be sent to Dulag-Luft at Wetzlar, the center from which prisoners were processed for dispatch to the established POW camps.

During the rail journey to Wetzlar, I pondered why Zemke had been let off the hook so easily. It appeared that I had only been subjected to the standard methods of interrogation which all Allied airmen received. Surely with my background the Luftwaffe interrogators would not pass me over so easily.

At Dulag-Luft the senior Allied officer was found to be Charles Stark, whom I had known prewar while serving at Langley Field, Virginia. Stark, now a colonel, had been shot down in the Mediterranean theater of operations the previous May and as a POW had the job of overseeing the distribution of International Red Cross supplies for Allied prisoners that came through Switzerland. Mostly these consisted of clothing to equip men for the rigors of prison camp life. Unfortunately, the supplies available never adequately met the needs of the prisoners. I was given a hand-knitted navy blue pullover, the work of and a donation from a lady in Boston, Massachusetts, to the Red Cross. This welcome garment became a bastion against winter chill and it was a rare occasion when it was not worn day or night.

There was also a need for some form of hat or cap to protect the head from winter weather, and as nothing was available from Red Cross sources, I set out to make my own. A pair of worn khaki trousers underwent radical modification to become a makeshift cap complete with ear flaps and served satisfactorily to keep the head warm. A further acquisition resulting from a favorable acquaintance with a supply sergeant was a used GI alpaca-lined jacket with hood.

With no regular duties, much of the time was passed with needle and thread embroidering a colonel's insignia on the shoulders of my jacket and homemade flight cap. While there were regular dispatches of small groups of POWs to prison camps, Zemke was not included. As the days dragged by I became increasingly apprehensive as to the reason for this delay. The Dulag-Luft staff could offer no explanation. Then, on the morning of 11 December, my worst fears were realized when I was ordered to report to the camp administrator's office; I was informed I was being returned to Auswertestelle-West under armed guard. The gloom at the prospect of further interrogation was lifted somewhat on the train journey south from Wetzlar. After boarding the train by the novel expedient of the toilet window as my guards sought to avoid the crush at the doors, I was seated beside a young German girl. At first the child, who was about ten years old, showed fear at the presence of the enemy prisoner and was amazed when I started to talk to her in her own language. After a while quite a rapport was established. The pleasant scene suddenly erupted into carnage. Bullets smashed into the carriage, killing one of the guards sitting opposite and nearly decapitating the small girl, whose body fell across my lap. As the train came to an abrupt halt the side of the carriage was blasted by an explosion. Instantly realizing Allied fighters were at work, I made a dash for the door to take shelter behind some railside rocks. The train was in mountainous terrain, with a river on one side and a steep rock cliff on the other. Between the fighters' strafing runs, I made trips to the carriages to help out the wounded. The hysterical mother of the little girl and another small sister were brought to safety. Having exhausted their ammunition and ordnance the attacking fighters departed.

After narrowly escaping death from my own side, I was now faced with another dangerous situation. As survivors emerged from hiding their fear had given way to anger which was now directed at me, one of the hated Terrorfliegers, a compatriot of those who had just brought death and devastation. The future did not look bright, particularly when a man was seen to pick up a length of splintered wood. At this moment a Wehrmacht lieutenant appeared, drew his pistol, and warned the crowd not to harm the prisoner. The German officer then ordered me to follow him down the track, leading the way to a farmhouse on the other side of the small river. Here I was held in one of the rooms, my surviving original guard eventually appearing to take charge.

In the same room was an attractive, well-groomed young woman who had been on the train. Judging by the attention she received, she was someone of importance. After several hours a staff car arrived and the lieutenant ordered my guard to sit beside the driver while he, the attractive woman, and the unkempt prisoner sat in the back seat. The driver was lacking either in experience or in aptitude for his performance was most erratic, he seemed to have difficulty in changing gear, and when told by the lieutenant to increase speed he wandered from side to side. The lieutenant kept a wary eye out for Allied fighter bombers and as we approached Frankfurt down the Autobahn he suddenly warned the driver to pull off the road. Panicking, the driver swerved sharply. The car left the road, turned on its side, and came to a stop at the bottom of an embankment with me on top of the pile in the back. After making an exit through the window, it was a pleasure to extract the lady. The lieutenant was uninjured but the guard suffered a bang on the head and the errant driver severe bruising and suspected fractures. No strafing attack developed as the P-38s the lieutenant spotted had flown past.

Darkness had fallen by the time we eventually reached the Oberursel camp. Next morning I found myself once again in the presence of Hanns

Scharff. My immediate question was why they had brought me back for interrogation. Scharff said quite improbably that an article in a United States magazine, following the report that Zemke was missing in action, had found its way to the German general staff, the OKW. They had not realized such a notorious airman had been captured and wanted to meet him.

I was driven to a house in the forest, a hunting lodge belonging to Georg von Opel, head of the Opel car firm. Heavily guarded, this place was apparently used for special purposes by the staff of Auswertestelle-West. Left to my own devices, I was able to have a long-desired hot bath and my clothes laundered by the lodge staff. This luxury was taken further by the provision of a three-course dinner, a nice bedroom, and clean sheets.

The following day senior German officers, identified by red stripes down their trouser legs, began to arrive. Gefreiter Scharff was present to make the introductions. It was apparent that this chief interrogator was no ordinary private first class as he appeared perfectly at ease in the company of generals and colonels, laughing and joking with them as if he was of equal rank. Wined and dined, I was very much on my guard. The object of this OKW interest in me became apparent when I was plied with questions on my attitude to Communists and the Soviets. It was put that the threat to western democracy really lay there, not with Germany; would I head a volunteer fighter organization composed of Allied and German fighter pilots to fight in the East? If interested the pay would be in gold, equivalent to 1,000 US dollars a month.

It was difficult to believe this was a serious proposition, particularly at this stage of the war. I could only suppose the generals were naive enough to think my Pomeranian-Bavarian ancestry might spark some sentiment for their cause. After my smiling refusal, I was then approached by Herr von Collande, who introduced himself as a playwright and film director, currently working on a documentary about Allied air operations. He wanted some technical assistance that did not involve classified matters. Again there would be a remuneration for services rendered. Declining, I realized that the basic purpose of this get-together was to try to ensnare a US officer into something that could be used for propaganda purposes by the Nazis. Even so, I was astounded at the apparent naivete of these men in trying to turn me traitor and concluded that the attempt revealed how desperate the Nazi situation must be.

Finding their efforts wasted, the Auswertestelle-West staff informed me I would be sent to Stalag Luft I at Barth, on the German Baltic coast. The choice was to be returned to Dulag-Luft to await the assembly of a POW party for that destination or, if my parole was given as an officer, to depart that day with a special escort directly to Barth. Not wishing to spend more uncertain days at Wetzlar, I chose the latter course.

My escort was a Luftwaffe lieutenant, and the first stage of our journey was a night train ride to Hanover, arriving early in the morning. There the usual long wait for a connection commenced, soon to be interrupted by the sounding of air raid sirens and adjournment to a shelter. Fate had taken us to Hanover rail station on the very day it had been selected as a target for 300 8th Air Force B-17s. Once more my buddies were putting my life in peril. A terrifying half hour was spent with other travelers as the massive concrete shelter was rocked by explosions. Although 900 tons of bombs were deposited on and around the station, reducing it to a smoking ruin, the shelter was spared a direct hit. The Luftwaffe lieutenant, anxious to deliver his charge to Barth, was advised by rail staff to follow the track out of the city—at first a difficult task as craters, twisted rails, and rubble barred the way. After a half mile or so we fell in with a small detachment of German soldiers also making their exodus from the blasted station. An incongruous spectacle resulted of a solitary Kriegsgefangener amidst a score of fully armed troops marching down the rail tracks. Eventually a passenger train was found in a small station and late in the day this departed for Berlin. Here a connection for Stralsund was sought but not found until another hour had been spent in a shelter, as RAF Mosquitoes pestered the enemy capital. Thereafter the journey to Barth was completed without real difficulty. Late in the afternoon of my third day of travel, Kriegsgefangener No. 6559, erstwhile fighter colonel, was confronted with the wired encampment that was to be his abode for many weeks.

2

Stalag Luft I

My first sight of Stalag Luft I's guard towers and high fences silhouetted against the darkening sky induced a strange feeling of relief. While having no desire to be imprisoned, I reasoned that for the first time since the day of my unintended arrival on German soil I was free of uncertainty. Here I would probably see out the rest of the war. The guards at the camp entrance inspected the papers presented by my escort and the outer gates were opened. Passing through this outer security check, I was taken to a barracks orderly room. Here a receipt was signed to my traveling guard relieving him of further responsibility. With a nod of his head and an "I wish you luck" he disappeared from the scene. After the usual fingerprinting and picture taking, two armed soldiers hustled me from reception and through another set of double gates surrounding an inner prison compound. Once more a series of signatures was needed to gain entrance.

By this time it was close to dark and prisoners were already confined in the low wooden buildings. Searchlights now blazed from watchtowers following our every step to one of the barracks. The guard unlocked a door and walked down a dimly lit passage to another door on which he gave a resounding knock. An American voice responded with a forceful "Enter." The guard opened the door and there, round a makeshift table, sat three smiling faces I knew well: Loren McCollom, Charles "Ross" Greening, and Mark E. Hubbard. All jumped to their feet yelling "Hub! Hub! Where the hell have you been? We've been waiting for you" and other welcoming remarks while pumping my hand and slapping my back. In the meantime the guards had departed, not unnoticed by Greening who dryly observed: "Oh, I forgot to tip them. What a shame. Remind me next time to be a bit more generous." After more banter a serious question was suddenly broached by all three. They wanted to know my date of rank. Why so important? "The thirteenth of May 1943," I replied, curious as to why they wanted to know. This brought much excitement, and while Mark Hubbard went dashing out of the room I was informed that I now rated the Senior Allied Officer in Stalag Luft I. Initially I did not appreciate the significance of this situation; not even when Hubbard returned with Colonel Jean Byerly, the current Senior Allied Officer, who through poor health was pleased to relinquish his position to me. At first demurring, I was finally convinced by my friends that I should not or could not escape the responsibility, and within an hour of my arrival I had signed the special order for the assumption of command of all Allied personnel in the camp. A certain bewilderment clouded my consciousness, engendered by all the information on life at Stalag Luft I which was heaped on me during the next few hours. However, it did not take long for the salient fact to sink in; I had fallen right into the hot seat of an extraordinary command of over 5,000 souls, something I didn't expect and most certainly wasn't looking for.

My three friends had learned of my impending arrival through the German administration and had prepared one of the four bunk beds in the small room for my occupation with—as Greening commented—a radio and all home comforts. On the wall backing this lower bunk Ross

Greening, an accomplished artist, had drawn a radio set with dials tuned to Hoaquin, a local station in Washington State. A snapshot had been fixed to this rendering of a radio. Bending down to look at it, I found the smiling faces of my wife, McCollom's, and Greening's. The snap had been taken during a get-together visit of the wives the summer before and had been sent to Greening, who now capitalized on the surprise effect it would have on me.

Byerly offered accommodation in his room, for which I thanked him, saying I would take up the subject on the morrow. For this night I would use the bunk already prepared for me and talk with my three old associates.

After Byerly had departed, much of the conversation centered on what had befallen each of us leading to our incarceration at Barth. Mark Hubbard had served with me at Langley Field in prewar days and was around the same age. A lieutenant colonel commanding the 20th Fighter Group for only two weeks before being shot down in a P-38 during an air fight in March 1944, Mark had previous combat experience in North Africa. Now as chief of staff of Provisional Wing X, the American prisoner organization in Stalag Luft I—the command that had just been sprung on me—he was, in effect, its center pin.

In the light of a flickering candle that first evening I learned how Mac McCollom, once my group executive in the 56th Fighter Group in England, had been lost. On his first dive-bombing mission with his new command, the 353rd Fighter Group, his P-47 had received a direct hit from an 88 mm shell over a small airfield just across the English Channel. The aircraft immediately burst into flames which enveloped the cockpit, and at the time it was thought Mac had perished. Somehow he managed to get out of that flaming wreck and now, a year later, the scars from the burns he received still showed on his hands and face as a pinky hue. This was especially so on cold days, I was told, and had led to his being stuck with a new nickname, Pinky. Mac now oversaw intelligence gathering in the US compounds of the camp and much of the undercover activities.

Of the three, the most unusual experiences were those of Ross Greening, who had been a fellow candidate for Air Corps cadet training in Portland,

Oregon, in 1935. Ross had flown with Jimmy Doolittle's force of B-25s that took off from carriers to bomb Tokyo. His bomber subsequently crashed in China. For four months he evaded capture behind Japanese lines before being rescued and sent back to the States. Ross was given command of the 17th Bomb Group, a B-26 outfit in North Africa, only to be shot down by flak over Naples a few weeks later. His parachute descent deposited him with a broken leg on Mount Vesuvius. Sent north to an Italian prison camp, he escaped in the confusion upon Italy's surrender. Making his way to Trieste, he joined Yugoslav partisans, only to be captured by the Germans and sent to work in a coal mine in Czechoslovakia. After much effort he finally convinced the authorities that he was a US officer and was then sent to his present abode. Ross was the commander of the prisoners in the North 1 compound, one of the four that made up the camp and the one in which I was placed.

In the course of our conversations, noticing a solitary electric light bulb hung from the ceiling of the room, I inquired why it was not illuminated. I learned that our captors extinguished lights at 1800 hours each evening and did not turn the power on again until morning. Fortunately the contents of the Red Cross parcels came in a very heavy waxed paper wrapping. When this paper was put in a bucket of hot water, the wax melted and floated to the surface; skimmed off and applied to strips of rag, it could be fashioned into effective candles. The soggy paper had its use as filler material for plugging cracks in walls and ceilings. My first introduction to the extraordinary ingenuity of prisoners of war.

We talked into the small hours of the night until fatigue overcame me. My clothing still on and a blanket wrapped around me for warmth, oblivion came quickly.

Not until the blowing of whistles early the next morning was I again aware of the world around. After washing my face in cold water and combing my hair, I was ushered out by my friends to stand with the rest of the prisoners in the open space that served as a parade ground. Here we were to be counted off by our guards; morning roll call, or *Appell* as it was called in German. Not since cadet days had I been required to report to a morning roll call. I was soon to discover that Appells were the demarkation points of the day, for this head count took place at 0645 hours and 1630 hours, rain or shine, snow or clear. The sullen POWs formed ranks, five deep, by barrack block with their designated barracks commander heading the show. The number of men in each block grouping varied from barracks to barracks, but I estimated that from the eleven in the compound some 1,500 prisoners were drawn up before the Luftwaffe compound officer—Lager officer—and his men. The military ritual observed that morning would vary little over the days and weeks to come.

Each barracks commander reported that his men were ready to be counted to the Allied compound commander, who in turn reported to the German Lager officer. The Lager officer then posted his guards at the front and rear to count the first block while the prisoners stood at attention. The count taken, this block again stood at ease. On completion of all block counts the Lager personnel huddled together to make their overall tally. If this was correct the Lager officer returned to the Allied compound commander and gave permission to dismiss the assembly. I observed that all this was done with military drill and, despite the assorted wear of the prisoners, with a fair amount of precision. In the cold of the north German winter nobody wanted to prolong this exercise if at all avoidable. In cases of illness the Germans went through every barracks counting the absentees by name. While they did this the cold and hungry prisoners on parade remained standing. The primary purpose of Appell was to check for possible escapes, although the German administration insisted that the count was necessary to establish numbers for rations and other requirements. On the command to dismiss, everyone made for his room to make a mug of barley coffee and to pull out a Red Cross box for whatever foodstuff had been saved from the previous day. One of the buildings in the compound served as a mess hall but no breakfast was served there, only the one hot meal of the day. From this first day it was apparent that food was the main topic of conversation. The reason was also clear; there wasn't anywhere near enough to satisfy even the smallest of POW appetites.

3

Prisoners' Problems

That Sunday, 17 December 1944, and the next few days were largely taken up with coming to terms with my new-found situation and responsibilities as well as learning the practice, problems, and secrets of the kriegie's world.

The camp had originally been opened in 1940 for captured RAF personnel. The site was probably chosen because of its remote position and high water table which could make escape tunneling difficult. By the following year it featured two compounds, one an Oflag for officers and the other a Stalag for what the British call "other ranks." The correct title of the camp was Kriegsgefangenerlager No 1 der Luftwaffe but it continued to be referred to as Stalag Luft I, this persisting even after it became designated as an officers-only camp.

In April 1942 all RAF prisoners were removed to other camps due to numerous escape attempts and the generally unsatisfactory state of the place. It was reopened in October that year when 200 RAF NCOs were transferred from Stalag Luft III, and it remained a true Stalag until November 1943. By this date the air assault on Hitler's empire had really begun to gather pace and the numbers of British and American airmen forced to alight in the enemy home and occupied lands increased, swamping the existing detention facilities. In a reorganization, all the RAF NCOs were transferred to the new Stalag Luft VI, Barth becoming an officers-only setup—apart from the NCOs who had volunteered to undertake orderly duties. A few USAAF men had been caged here during the early part of 1943 but now Americans came like a flood, initially into the South compound, which was later amalgamated with the West. From February 1944 US newcomers went into the new North 1 compound. This was soon overcrowded and work on two more compounds was begun: North 2, opening at the beginning of October, and North 3, which started to take in POWs about three weeks before my arrival and was still being constructed.

The main, or original, compound was generally known as the West because of its position in relation to the Vorlager, the compound which contained the German administrators' buildings, the hospital, workshops, and stores. The West compound held the most kriegies, around 1,400 US and 890 British and other Allied prisoners at the time I became SAO (Senior Allied Officer). North 1, my "home," had over 1,500 men and North 2 nearly 1,400. The new North 3 had just 78 inhabitants. All but a handful in the North compounds were USAAF people.

The largest compound, the West, had latrines and tapped water in the barracks as also had North 1, said to have been originally constructed for and used by Hitler Youth until being absorbed into the prison complex. These two compounds each had a large communal building with kitchen and mess facilities that also served as a theater and recreational room. North 2 and North 3 were far more austere, having few facilities and the latrines and washhouses being separate buildings. At this time there were seven barracks in North 2 and two in North 3 with five more being constructed. All barracks were of rough-cut lumber construction with a central corridor and small dormitory rooms of various sizes on either side, the largest 18 by 24 feet. Each barracks hut was built on wooden studs so that there was between one and two feet of clearance between the floor and the ground. This was done to facilitate searches by the Germans for tunnels, but it had the effect of making the huts much colder as air could circulate underneath. There was just about enough room for dogs to move around below. Generally, a *Hundführer* with two vicious German shepherds roamed inside each locked compound all night. Sleeping accommodation was double or triple stacked wooden bunks, and mattresses were filled with wood shavings. The stoves for heating and cooking varied in size and capacity; they were all completely inadequate as far as providing warmth was concerned. All barracks windows had shutters on the outside which the guards closed at specified times once the prisoners were locked up for the night. The rooms were originally lit by powerful electric bulbs until in the cause of electricity saving—the excuse the Germans gave—these were replaced by bulbs that gave only feeble illumination. While the changes were carried out some agile POW minds quickly worked a plan to take the new low-power bulbs from the first installations and run ahead and substitute them for high-power bulbs in the rooms the Germans had yet to reach. In this way low-power bulbs replaced low-power bulbs in several barracks until the Germans caught on to what was happening.

Each compound was enclosed by double ten-foot-high barbed wire fences, and although there were intercommunicating gates these were normally kept locked. Surrounding the whole camp was another double barbed wire fence with guard towers at strategic intervals. Searchlights mounted on these towers illuminated the whole perimeter at night.

The layout of the camp was a reverse L-shape, more or less following the natural contours of the bay estuary to the west. Located on a low-lying Baltic peninsula covered with pine woods and scrubland, Stalag Luft I was fairly well isolated from the civilian population. But the whole area had a military presence that was in complete disregard of the international agreement that prison camps should not be so located. Alongside West compound was a Luftwaffe antiaircraft artillery school where young gunners—both men and women—trained in the skills that would increase the numbers of incarcerated Allied airmen. On the other side of the bay area there was some sort of chemical warfare experimental station, and about two miles south of us lay an airfield around which little flying activity was noted. We discovered later that aircraft assembly was carried on here by slave labor. Some components for this work were secreted away in the scrub directly north of our camp.

My own experience during just a few weeks of captivity had demonstrated how a lack of food and warmth can have a dampening effect upon the morale of the individual. While the Germans certainly had their problems with food at this stage in the war, the only thing to be said for that supplied to Stalag Luft I POWs was that it kept men from starving. Without doubt hunger was intentionally induced with the aim of subduing the internees. The German food was prepared in a central kitchen by the POW volunteers and distributed to the compounds once a day. For the most part it consisted of vegetables—potatoes, turnips, and various sorts of beet and cabbage. Occasionally there would be a small piece of horsemeat. A thin barley soup and black bread were fairly regular features of the menu. Fortunately there were Red Cross food parcels to supplement the German rations, each prisoner normally being issued one per week. Every parcel had about a dozen different foodstuffs in cans or packs plus soap and cigarettes. The canned meats, sardines, jams, and candies provided the necessary extra nourishment for our diet, as well as giving amateur cooks the opportunity to try and make the prison rations more palatable.

The Red Cross also provided blankets and uniform clothing, although such was the influx of new prisoners during the summer and fall of 1944 that there was now a shortage. The Germans supplied no clothing and had been known to take away items of US uniform that they considered too closely resembled civilian wear and thus violated camp security regulations. Currently, few prisoners were adequately clothed to endure the winter weather that prevailed in this area.

I was briefed that the camp Kommandant, Oberst (Colonel) Scherer, was an ardent Nazi, as were several members of his staff. In recent months the attitude toward prisoners had hardened, with the imposition of restrictive regulations backed by the threat of severe punishment on infringement. Even the Senior Allied Officer was not immune from harsh treatment. Colonel William Hatcher, who filled the post in January 1944, after his command of an 8th Air Force bomb group had been terminated by flak over Bordeaux, had been transferred to another camp for continually protesting about the poor conditions in Stalag Luft I. Jean Byerly, a B-17 group commander in Italy before capture late in 1943, took his place.

It was under Byerly's leadership that in the spring of 1944 an overall POW organization was formed within the camp. This met with partial German acceptance as the advertised aim was to effect order and discipline in a military manner. To be known as Provisional Wing X, its stated purpose was the administration of all internal affairs, communication with Red Cross and YMCA representatives, POW discipline, the maintenance of records on all POWs, particularly those concerning health, and to organize the evacuation of the camp when that time came. There were, of course, other reasons for establishing such an organization, not least the subjective effect it would come to have in making the German administration acknowledge that the prisoners had an authority to be reckoned with; for the aim was to create a headquarters that could speak as one voice for all the prisoners. While for practical reasons at this time it was agreed the British and American contingents should be administered separately with close liaison, the Senior Allied Officer and a selected staff in North 1 would form the Headquarters of Provisional Wing X.

Each compound would be organized as a group and each barracks as a squadron with the respective officers in charge heading these commands. No doubt the imposition of this quasi-military setup was not viewed favorably by all POWs, particularly those individuals who tried to avoid anything that had to do with discipline or order. The majority, however, quickly recognized that this was not senior officers playing at military bureaucracy but a way to bring some strength into our dealings with our captors. And it was soon evident to me also that this organization, which I now commanded, had worthwhile purposes and achievements.

In accepting the responsibilities of Senior Allied Officer I was con-
forming to the policy established for prison camps, which meant that
Jean Byerly became my deputy, the chief of staff for Provisional Wing X.
Byerly's chronic liver ailment had gradually impeded his ability to fulfill
his duties as Senior Allied Officer. The harsh living conditions only
aggravated this disorder, for it proved impossible to provide him with the
necessary diet to effect improvement. Lieutenant Colonel George
Hankey, who headed the small British medical team that worked unceas-
ingly to provide some sort of medical service for all POWs, did his best
for Byerly although handicapped by lack of medicines and inadequate
facilities.

Because his ill health frequently confined him to his room or bed for
many days at a time, Byerly was more or less my deputy in name only.
His duties fell to Mark Hubbard, who had previously acted as chief of
staff, with the able assistance of our adjutant, Captain Milton Zahn.
Although our paths had crossed before, it was only now that I came to
appreciate the astuteness of Mark Hubbard, not least for his quick grasp
of a given problem. He frequently had the answer before I completed the
question! An excellent man at his job and difficult to stay ahead of. I had
not encountered Zahn before and learned that he entered captivity after
leaving the cockpit of a stricken 8th Air Force B-17. This man possessed
a near photographic memory and could quote Army regulations to the
letter. A born administrator and able clerk, he produced the necessary
paperwork from the lone typewriter provided the Wing Headquarters—
or as the kriegies called it, the Head Shed.

Just like an Air Force headquarters, we had four staff sections. A-1,
which handled personnel records, was the province of Major Dillingham;
McCollom handled A-2, intelligence; Major Todd movements, educa-
tion, and athletics under A-3; while A-4, supply, under Captain Birkner,
dealt with the issue and receiving of Red Cross and YMCA supplies. The
American compound commanders were Ross Greening for North 1,
Lieutenant Colonel Cy Wilson, another one-time CO of the 20th Fighter
Group, in North 2, Lieutenant Colonel Francis Gabreski, former prom-
inent member of my old 56th, in North 3, and for the US contingent

in West compound, Colonel Einar Malstrom, a former CO of the 356th
Fighter Group. As I could not visit the other compounds without special
permission and an armed guard, for the time being I was prevented from
meeting the other compound commanders.

I learned that the previous senior officer in North 2 had been Colonel
Henry "Russ" Spicer, whom I recalled as the distinctive commander of
the 357th Group, one of the first Mustang outfits when I was leading the
56th. Spicer's distinction was that in contrast to most American fliers his
face bore a moustache—an RAF handlebar type at that. Following a
morning Appell, Spicer had addressed his compound assembly on the
finer points of what he would like to do with his captors in view of their
uncharitable actions. Overheard by the Lager staff, he was later removed
to the camp prison to stand trial on trumped-up mutiny charges. The
Senior British Officer, Group Captain Marwood-Elton, and one of his
senior staff, Wing Commander R. C. M. Ferres, had been arrested on
similar charges back in August 1944 and were awaiting trial at Stralsund,
a large town to the east of Barth. Both men had previously attempted
escapes and were obviously intent on making things as difficult for their
captors as possible. Marwood-Elton was to face a court on a charge of
incitement to mutiny, for which the maximum sentence was death. A
ridiculous charge; the real reason for his arrest was probably that somehow the Germans had learned he was actively engaged in collecting
useful intelligence and briefing repatriates from the camp to carry this to
England.

On the first day after my arrival in camp Colonel Byerly had been
thanked for his offer to share his room and told I had decided to remain,
at their invitation, with my three old friends. Thus Room 21, Block 9,
North Compound 1 became my residence for the uncertain days that lay
ahead. The company was the only attraction, for the room was just as
spartan as all others in the compound. Approximately 12 by 10 feet, with
a solitary window exposing the nearby barbed wire fences and a stand of
pines beyond. Four wooden bunks lined one wall, while in the opposite
inner corner sat a small iron stove. A small cardboard box beside it contained the few precious coal brickets that served as fuel, while a battered

water-heating container was a near permanent resident on top of the stove. A rickety board nailed to the wall alongside served as a kitchen cabinet where a few spoons, knives, forks, cups, and dinner plates reposed; these, together with a small metal pot, being the total kitchenware. Furniture consisted of the small wooden table, one chair, and two stools. If a guest visited, someone had to sit on a bunk bed. No lockers or cupboards were provided; so a Red Cross box under a bed served as a personal storage place. A few sundry items of clothing hung from nails in the walls. Nothing in the room showed any sign of having been painted and every crack in the boarded walls had been stuffed with paper to hold out the cold. On the floor pieces of cardboard served as mats to keep wood splinters out of feet. It did occur to me that I'd seen better hovels in hobo camps back home.

The Senior Allied Officer was accorded no special privileges in day-to-day living. My three roommates shared housekeeping and cooking duties by rotation and I was now included. Every fourth day it was my turn to serve as chef. After burning the first meal attempted, I was summarily dismissed from further culinary pursuits and permanently relegated to washing and wiping dishes and clearing the table. Greening excelled at the cooking stove, an art acquired from his time with underground forces. He, best of all, could turn out a tasty morsel that slid down the throat with ease.

Unlike my previous military appointments, this one offered no shortage of time to meditate upon the problems of command. During those first days at Barth I thought hard and long about the situation. The Senior Allied Officer could be no more than a figurehead and mouthpiece for the POW organization, but that was not to my satisfaction. It was reasoned that the overriding aim must be the welfare of the prisoners and to see that when the day of liberation came all, or as many as possible, were still alive and well. Despite the new Wehrmacht offensive in the west the Third Reich would surely crumble before next summer. There was frequent speculation in the camp as to what would happen in the last throes of the Nazi regime. Some thought the Germans would exterminate us as a last act of spite. I did not consider this a serious possibility but did expect the Allied POWs to be used as hostages in some attempt to bargain. Whatever happened, our best chance of survival lay in our own preparedness for any eventuality. Thus it was my objective to strengthen the POW organization by every means available and at the same time to get the German camp administration to recognize it as an efficient setup to be reckoned with.

I had already been amazed by many of the enterprises being success-fully pursued in the camp, much unknown to our captors. The ability to tackle just about anything was not so surprising when one considered that we had more than 5,000 men drawn from all walks of life and all trades and professions. This abundance of talents, handicapped by the serious restraints of confinement as it was, should still have been able to outwit the Luftwaffe staff and the sulking guards. While they attempted to subjugate and condition us to accepting our servitude, we had to strive to keep them under pressure at every opportunity to sustain our own morale and crack theirs. Such objectives were undoubtedly those of my predecessors, which I now intended to pursue with the same determina-tion. It was only natural that the old hands would resent any interference from this upstart newcomer, a situation to which I was sensitive. Time should bring acceptance, and for now it would be prudent not to interfere with established procedures.

While it was vital that our keepers should be encouraged to see the prisoners as a well-organized and disciplined body of men rather than as a helpless collection of humanity, we also had to work on those Germans who were either sympathetic to us and disillusioned with their own masters or just plain corruptible. This aim, of course, had been pursued with vigor long before I arrived on the scene. As Senior Allied Officer I saw my part in the scheme of things as one of sizing up the senior Ger-man administrators and working on those who showed signs of sym-pathy. A first move was to request an introductory meeting with the Kommandant. This was arranged for the regular Monday morning meeting that he had with British and American senior officers. Here I also met my British counterpart for the first time, Wing Commander "Freddie" Hilton.

When the influx of US prisoners commenced early in 1944, the British and American Senior Officers had agreed that the highest ranking officer prisoner in the camp, whatever his nationality, should become the designated Senior Allied Officer. Such a position was desirable in order for the POWs to present a united front in dealing with the camp administration. The British, understandably, wanted to continue to run their own affairs, but there was a close liaison between the SBO and SAO on all important matters. The British, having been first on the scene, were also the chief instigators and operators of the various underground activities, although US personnel were now fully involved.

The Kommandant or his representative also came to North 1 every Wednesday afternoon for a meeting with the Senior Allied Officer. Matters to be raised by the POWs had to be submitted in writing before the meetings. Most of our requests concerned seemingly mundane matters such as the provision of extra light bulbs, repair of a phonograph, a shortage of knives and forks, and the like. As my colleagues in Provisional Wing X had warned me, most of these requests were refused, often without reasonable explanation. Our hard-hearted would-be masters did relent over Christmas services, with permission for movement between some Lagers on the giving of paroles not to try to escape. In contrast to my lack of supporters—only the adjutant or a clerk could be present—the German staff usually appeared in strength at these meetings. Initially, I was aware that apart from Scherer himself, authority issued from a Major Schröder, who headed the Lager personnel, and Major von Miller zu Aichholz in charge of camp security. Both, I had been warned, were committed Nazis; von Miller in particular was detested for his actions against the POWs, especially in search and seizure raids.

After only a couple of meetings new faces appeared in the camp administration. For reasons unknown to me, Scherer was transferred out and his place as Kommandant taken by an older man, Oberst von Warnstedt. At the same time there appears to have been a general shake-up in the staff, for other Luftwaffe officers disappeared, including Schröder. Unfortunately the infamous von Miller remained to head the Abwehr detachment of security police.

With the changed administration came new and ominous regulations. A new German order, issued soon after New Year's Day, warned that in future any prisoner touching a compound warning wire would be shot at without challenge. The warning wire was a single strand that ran knee-high round the inside of all compounds just inside the double barbed wire fence. As in the course of playing ball games or exercising it was quite easy for a prisoner to accidentally brush against the wire, this decree looked very much like a license for the guards to shoot at will. In another notice the new Lager Gruppenleiter (head of Lager personnel) Oberstleutnant Jäger announced the discontinuation of the Monday meetings between senior Allied officers and the Kommandant, leaving only the Wednesday afternoon visit as a means of contact. Even more ominous in our minds was another requirement that all prisoners, both British and American, of the Jewish faith were to be housed in separate barracks in North 1. This was not the end of impositions making life more difficult for POWs. Officers were ordered to give up part of their bed linen so that this could be used by new prisoners who continued to arrive in large numbers, many removed from Stalag Luft IV at Gross Tychow to the east which was threatened by the Russian advance. Much furniture was also appropriated for use elsewhere. More serious was that deliveries of foodstuffs from German sources, notably potatoes, started to arrive late, sometimes a week overdue, causing reductions in daily rations. Additionally, a limit was put on the amount of food that an individual could save and store from his Red Cross parcels. Similarly the reserve of canned jam and other foods held by central compound stores was confiscated—and this at a time when the supply of Red Cross parcels held for the camp was down to a two weeks' supply. These inflictions, coming one after another, showed clearly that the new regime was deliberately turning the screw on our containment. Whether it was of their own volition or at the direction of higher authority we had no way of telling.

Our immediate recourse was to write to the Representative of our Protecting Power, which happened to be the Swiss legation in Germany, protesting that our jailers had violated articles in the Geneva Convention. The representative visited the camp every six months and, as he had been there just two days before my arrival, was not scheduled again until April. In the letter we requested that the seriousness of the matters outlined required an immediate visit. Although the Germans, as signatories to the 1929 Geneva Convention on the rights of prisoners of war, were obliged to forward the letter, on past showing it was likely they would sit on it for a month or so—which they did.

Faced with this oppression, it was in the nature of the prisoners to show defiance in any way they could. While the Headquarters staff of Provisional Wing X would secretly encourage and support this resistance, it was important that they maintain what dialogue there was with our oppressors. Protest and demand, but never stoop to measures that would discredit our standing as the mouthpiece and authority of the POWs. In consequence I did not lose an opportunity to request an audience with the Kommandant.

While the majority of our grievances were turned aside and I had to rely on the one weekly meeting to get my points across, gradually it did seem they were receiving more attention, even if mostly in the negative sense. Despite the harsh regulations he had imposed, or been instructed to impose, von Warnstedt did not appear to be a hard-core Nazi disciplinarian. One distinct advantage I had was being able to converse in German, if haltingly, as this allowed direct exchanges with the Kommandant avoiding the filtering of an interpreter. He came over as a man who was not enthusiastic about the job he held down, the more so because other members of his staff appeared to speak for him or he would pass my question to one of them. In fact, I had an inkling that he was a little disenchanted with the war and, if I sensed correctly, he was not the only member of his staff so affected.

4

Kriegies' Secret World

Undoubtedly the failure of the Wehrmacht's major offensive in the west—which has come to be called the Battle of the Bulge—must have convinced many more Germans that the war was lost. This offensive, launched at the date of my arrival in Stalag Luft I, came at a time when many prisoners thought the Third Reich was about to topple, with liberation just around the corner. They found this unexpected German push a depressing setback. Our German administrators were quick to play up what was, for once, good news for them in the bulletin they pinned up daily in each compound. Based on Goebbels's propaganda, it was generally a source of amusement to POWs, who noted these bulletins were always a bit vague on the matter of German retreats and other adverse situations.

The POW community had for some time countered this propaganda with a daily news sheet of their own. A year previously the RAF men, with German approval, had started a camp newspaper which contained news culled from German newspapers and radio broadcasts plus information from new arrivals. Issued daily, a sufficient number of copies were made on an office typewriter to enable a copy to be distributed to each barrack, where someone read it to those who were interested. The compilers ignored items they recognized as propaganda and also took care not to include anything that might provoke their captors into banning the news sheet. This innocuous publication also helped to give cover to another, secret, daily news sheet. Much to my amazement, the main source of information was the BBC news broadcasts listened to twice daily—at 1300 and 2100 hours—on secret radios. At the time I knew little about this activity and for security's sake did not want to know. Only after the war were the details learned.

The radios were in the West compound, where the designated listeners took down the BBC news in longhand and passed it to the West compound security officer, Squadron Leader D. J. Kilgallin, who hid the notes in a tin of dried milk that had been fitted with a false bottom. Kilgallin waited until after morning Appell and, if there were no barracks searches by the Germans, he first dictated the latest BBC bulletins to a typist who made a copy on the smallest sheet of paper that would take it all. Any very thin paper obtained was kept for this purpose. While communication between compounds was only allowed with special permission, the camp authorities did permit a daily trip of the official liaison officer appointed to carry open messages and papers between the Senior British Officer in West compound and myself, the Senior Officer in North 1. This liaison officer was Warrant Officer R. R. Drummond, RAF; he also carried in the transcript of BBC news and, although often searched, was never apprehended by the Germans. The hiding place was Drummond's wristwatch, from which the works had been removed; but he was still able to adjust the hands to give the time of day when he passed inspection by the compound guards.

Once inside my barracks building he went to the room occupied by First Lieutenant D. MacDonald. Drummond read the BBC news to MacDonald and immediately burned the copy he had carried. MacDonald then prepared a single sheet in American style based on the BBC news related to him. This was called the *POW-WOW*; only four typed copies of each issue were produced, one for each of the North compounds and the US contingent in the West. The British produced their own write-up of the BBC news which they called *Red Star*. Each copy of the secret news sheet was distributed to POW barracks security officers, who usually arranged for the reader of the approved camp newsletter to read also the BBC news to the men gathered in the barracks for their midday snack. The *POW-WOW* was read first because it was of more interest, but should the Germans suddenly arrive the reader could quickly return to the camp newspaper. After being read out, all *POW-WOW* copies quickly ended up in stoves so no evidence of their existence remained.

The lack of free movement for prisoners between the compounds was a major obstacle to distribution, and the way this was overcome was another example of POW ingenuity. On my first days walking in the compound I had noticed that people were often to be seen milling around, apparently aimlessly, trying to shake off the boredom. Some men would pick up stones and throw at some makeshift target. This was not as casual or impromptu as it first appeared, but rather a planned operation to condition the guards to the normality of the act. The purpose was to help conceal the method of communication between the compounds, and in particular the distribution of the *POW-WOW*. Copies were carefully wrapped around stones and thrown over the North 1 wire into North 2 when lookouts detailed to watch the towers and walking guards gave the all-clear to the pitcher. A designated receiver would intercept each missile before it hit the ground. In a similar operation one of the copies would be passed on to North 3 from North 2.

The West compound presented a much more difficult problem as the German-occupied part of the camp lay between it and North 1. This was solved by the cooperation of Second Lieutenant J. K. Lash, our postal officer. The authorities allowed a courier to pick up the incoming and outgoing mail from each compound every day. He moved with a guard and was liable to be searched. The single typewritten sheet was therefore carefully packed in wax paper wrapping and located in Lash's mouth between his teeth and cheek. The instructions were to chew the document up if he felt its safety was compromised. Lash delivered the *POW-WOW* for months without trouble. Had he been caught there is no doubt he would have spent the rest of his days at Stalag Luft I in the camp jail.

The Germans did, however, know of the existence of the *POW-WOW*. During one of their searches in the summer of 1944 they discovered a copy hidden in the room of Lowell Bennett, a US civilian journalist who had been shot down in an RAF bomber. It didn't take the Germans long to figure out the information could only have come from a BBC broadcast and that there must be a radio receiver in the camp. They promptly carried out very intensive searches of North 1, being convinced that the radio was in this compound, particularly after they found some hidden items associated with radio equipment. It turned out that this was not the setback it first seemed, for it helped to divert attention from the West compound where the radios were really hidden. North 1 was subject to the most frequent searches until the end of the war.

I had no idea where the radio was hidden or that there were two. The first had been constructed by two RAF men, mainly from smuggled parts, soon after Stalag Luft I became an officers-only late in 1943. At first operated on the camp electrical system, it was converted to run on flashlight batteries in order to listen to the BBC night broadcast when the camp electricity supply had been cut off. The receiver was concealed within a wall panel located behind a bed in the barrack room, some of the fixing nails acting as terminals to which an aerial wire and earphone cables could be attached. A second radio, a German civilian set, was obtained by a British Army private working in North compound as an orderly, but whose undercover task was to "encourage" a particular German to talk. When received, the set was found to be faulty, and as North compound could not get it to function it was smuggled in to the West compound inside a large soap box for the RAF radio experts to work on. When eventually brought into operation, this set was hidden in the camp theater behind a false cupboard back.

There was another source of news from outside, the Voice of America broadcasts, but these were principally listened to for another reason.

Around the time of D-Day a US flier had arrived in Stalag Luft I and informed Jean Byerly that he had been specially briefed on encoded messages for POWs contained in the Voice of America programs. Byerly passed this information to his British counterpart, who instructed the signals officer in West compound to arrange to have these broadcasts monitored. They took place from 0200 to 0230 daily, but as some modification had to be made to the radio it was not until mid-August 1944 that the Voice of America was successfully picked up. One or other of the operators, RAF Warrant Officers Hurrell and Kilminster, tuned into this program every night until 13 May 1945, only missing out on one or two occasions due to radio faults or poor conditions for reception. So that the messages could be decoded it was necessary that a verbatim record be made of each program. Lieutenant L. V. Trouve, a USAAF officer expert at shorthand, was moved into the barracks where the radio was hidden. To ease his load, the shorthand duties were later shared with Flight Lieutenant A. Small, a Canadian, and between them, working alternate nights, they recorded in full every Voice of America program that could be received.

A problem for the radio operators was being woken before 0200 hours when these broadcasts were scheduled. What was required was an alarm clock, an unlikely possession on any captured warrior. As luck would have it, a British Army orderly did have such a clock, but it was broken. One of the radio operators made a successful repair and muffled the alarm so it could not be heard more than a few feet away. The radio operator for the night kept the clock on a shelf above his bed and when the alarm sounded and awoke him, he raised the shorthand writer.

The shorthand script was transcribed into longhand early each morning and then handed to Lieutenant Colonel McKenzie, the US security officer in West compound. He had the means to decode the messages hidden in the transcript. His findings went first to the Senior British Officer who, if he considered the message had some relevance to our camp, arranged for it to be written on a tiny piece of paper and conveyed to North compound by Drummond in his works-less wristwatch.

It so happened that throughout my time as the SAO of Stalag Luft I there were no messages received via the Voice of America that were of particular significance to us. Only a very few of us knew about these broadcasts, and the knowledge that if the Allied headquarters did want to pass us specific instructions it could be done was certainly a boost to the morale of those in the know.

Escape was a subject that occupied the thoughts and activities of many detainees. An escape committee had been formed in the original compounds that became the West during the early days of RAF NCO occupation, and much of the expertise and escape material was passed on when Stalag Luft I became an officers-only camp. When the North compound was opened for US officers, the Germans were persuaded to transfer a few seniors from the original compounds to assume administrative duties for the new POWs. The real purpose was to ensure that the expertise and materials for escape and other clandestine prisoner activities were known and available. As a result, North compound was able to get its own escape show on the road almost immediately. Eventually, McCollom was appointed to coordinate all clandestine activities in the US compounds.

Despite the large number of attempts to flee Stalag Luft I, few had managed it successfully and, as far as was known, none got completely away. McCollom's section tried to exert some influence on the escape business through a secret committee that approved or rejected proposals. Escape had been attempted by many a method and ruse, but the farthest anyone had gotten from Barth was 36 miles before recapture. In fact, over 90 attempts had been made without success—mostly by the British, who took least kindly to confinement of all nationalities present. Tunnels had been a major activity since the camp was opened. The spit of land on which Stalag Luft I was sited had predominantly sandy soil, and though digging wasn't difficult, cave-ins were considered to be a hazard to tunnelers. In practice it was found that if lateral tunnels were shaped elliptically in cross-section there was little risk of cave-in and need for shoring. The tunnels were just large enough for a man to squiggle along on his belly using his elbows for propulsion. A major problem was the high water table of the area, particularly during the winter months when even the most shallow workings were flooded.

After the failure of every tunnel enterprise during the past year it was realized that the Germans had installed seismographic equipment to fix on underground noises. Von Miller must have smiled to himself every time a tunnel project started, allowing the prisoners to slave away with makeshift tools, use scarce shoring boards (stolen bed slats) on the vertical shafts, manufacture bellows, install air ducting, and carefully dispose of dirt in the exercise area. When the tunnel neared the inner fence his men would pounce. The Abwehr deliberately permitted such tunneling to continue until nearing completion simply to frustrate and dishearten prisoners. In the summer and early fall three tunnels had been attempted; two had failed but the third was thought to have missed detection. Work proceeded and the run reached outside the North 1 compound. Then the Abwehr suddenly appeared, drove a steel rod down directly into the tunnel, which was then opened up and the scruffy miners escorted to a month's stretch of solitary confinement on sour black bread and water.

Other prisoners tried to get away by deception. Perhaps the most ingenious ruse was one that found a kriegie moving out disguised as a Russian prisoner, a party of whom came regularly under guard to remove refuse from each compound. Though successfully mingling with the Russians and passing from our camp to theirs, he was tripped up next morning when the Germans found an extra Russian worker during a head count. Another bold effort involved simulating one of our POW crews which the Germans used for fetch and carry work outside the camp. These were enlisted men, as the Geneva Convention held that officers were not to work for their captors. Complete with men disguised as escorts, the party marched from their compound successfully, only to have an alert guard on the main gate check that no work parties were scheduled out on that particular day. Probably the most unlucky escape of which I heard was that of a Canadian squadron leader who hid in a sack to which a great many empty food cans had been attached. Placed in the tin disposal box, he was later carried out to the tin dump by fellow prisoners. While the guards' attention was distracted, the escapee was tipped out to become part of the tin pile and to wait for darkness before emerging from the sack. That evening a German soldier came looking for a tin and against all the odds tried to pick up one that was attached to the sack, thus discovering the POW.

Perhaps the easiest, if most dangerous, escape procedure entailed manufacturing a pair of wire cutters and snipping at the barbed wire that contained us. The danger lay in the risk that if detected the guards would open fire without a challenge. On a stormy black night one or two courageous lads would slip under the warning wire, crawl to the fence and, when the walking guard moved away or was deliberately distracted by noises, start cutting their way through. The primary difficulty of this method was a mass of coiled wire between the double fence, but once the escapees were in this wire they were difficult to spot. Having cut through, they had a dash to a nearby wood or the bullrush swamps on the edge of the bay of not much more than 100 yards at the nearest point.

Once clear, the problems really mounted. The escapee had to be provided with some sort of civilian disguise, money, identity cards, and maps to have much hope of success. The Germans all carried identity cards and often special work and travel permits. With the number of security and police checks, the escapee had to have a well-thought-out plan, ultra courage, and some knowledge of the language and customs of the country. A measure of luck had to prevail too. The camp escape committees grilled those involved on their plans to try to highlight weaknesses, because there were just too few resources to expend on any but the well-thought-out and practical plan.

The location of Barth made any attempt by an escapee to travel west almost certain of failure. Going east to the Russian lines offered more hope but was fraught with problems. One plan proposed was for a band of prisoners to steal a fishing boat from a nearby port and sail to neutral Sweden. This was reviewed by the escape committee and turned down, mainly on the improbability of being able to get several people away from the camp in one effort to crew such a venture.

Considering that every failed escape probably provided the Abwehr with more knowledge on the subject and enabled them to better counter future attempts, the chances of gaining freedom this way became more unlikely. No doubt they were up to most of our tricks and many of the prohibitive regulations imposed on us were devised to make escape more difficult, in particular by denying us access to materials from which escape aids might be fashioned. With the prospect of an Allied victory that surely could not be far away, I came to the conclusion that our meager resources could at this stage be better employed on the welfare of the whole camp rather than supporting a few individuals in attempts that were almost certain to fail.

In West compound the Senior British Officer had already forbade further attempts at escape. In the fall the Germans had posted notices warning against escape attempts into what they hinted was now a forbidden zone where any unauthorized person apprehended could be shot. This looked like another excuse to kill, and with Germany's defeat imminent—or so it seemed at the time—escaping was seen as an unnecessary risk. However, our uncertain future resulted in the decision to dig an emergency tunnel that would only be used in very dire circumstances. The work was carried out under the direction of a US officer in West compound and the tunnel extended well out beyond the boundary wire when completed. Happily there was never need to use it and the Abwher never knew of its existence. One can only guess they had ceased using their detection equipment.

Considerable effort had been expended on making equipment and other aids for the purposes of escape. Organized sections tackled such difficult work as making wire cutters out of stolen ice skate blades, garments that looked like enemy uniforms or civilian clothes, and, probably most exacting of all, forging printed material. Mostly done by hand, this included camp passes, travel permits, ration cards, identification papers, and labor cards for foreign workers. Just how good this work was is illustrated by the three US officers who, dressed as Germans, tried to walk out of the Vorlager gate using forged passes. The guards weren't fooled but they thought the passes had been stolen until subjecting them to close examination. As a result new gate passes were issued with a most complex design on the reverse side. It was only a matter of a few weeks before the new pass had been obtained and successfully reproduced.

Obtaining the real documents and passes to copy was in itself one of the most difficult problems. During my residence in the camp most material of this nature was obtained from cooperative Germans, disillusioned with the Nazis and fearful of the oncoming Russians. In the past the main source had been contacts in the hospital at Neubrandenburg, to which POWs had been sent for special medical treatment. Patients who returned to Stalag Luft I reported that many of the nursing orderlies were Poles. The enterprising Flight Lieutenant Delarge, himself a Pole and fluent in a number of languages, feigned an illness that would ensure his removal to Neubrandenburg. While there he recruited the services of two Poles and a former French Army officer in obtaining material and information. After his return most POWs who went for treatment at this hospital were briefed beforehand on how to contact these helpers without arousing suspicion. This proved to be the most useful source of contact with outside sympathizers in the area.

A duplicating process was devised, using table jelly sent in Red Cross food parcels. Then, in the summer of 1944, I.S.9, the agency set up by the British in the UK to monitor and communicate with POW camps, was able to get a camera into the camp. It proved to be far more effective in duplicating the forgeries. Again, it was only after the war that I learned the camera had been hidden in a chimney stack in West compound. A brick had been taken from the stack and a wood box, of the same dimensions and capable of taking the camera, fitted in place. The faces of the brick had been carefully sliced off and fixed to the exposed part of the box. Another hiding place never discovered.

Escape aid was only one of many secret activities of Pinky's organization, which had workers, known as the Saints, in many areas of the camp, some engaged in quite hair-raising activities. In addition to two secret radio receivers, I learned that we also had a Morse transmitter and could send emergency messages to an Allied source. Only a handful of people knew of their existence and where they were successfully hidden. McCollom would have told me where but I did not want to know. The fewer secrets a man held the better.

Also secret and even more intriguing to me was just how this equipment was obtained. Once more, not until after hostilities did I learn that

Allied agents had intercepted next-of-kin and YMCA parcels and secreted components in the contents. While I was Senior Allied Officer all such parcels came from the USA. Over a hundred carrying contraband were received during 1944 and 1945 and I do not know of any from this source being intercepted. This may seem incredible, particularly as the Germans suspected material was being smuggled into the camp this way and had actually discovered escape material in a box of British Christmas crackers in December 1943. The crackers had been badly packed and the box fell apart. A German picked up a cracker and invited a bystander to pull it. When the cracker came apart they were just a little surprised to see German money and maps come floating out.

The major factor in successfully hiding this and other clandestine activity was the large number of POWs. The Germans had around 500 men to contain us but only a small proportion were on duty at one time and they could not possibly observe all POW activity. We had the advantage of numbers when it came to outwitting the camp authorities; parcel sorting was a good example of this.

It was permissible for next of kin to send clothing, sports items and games, books, cigarettes, tobacco, and food. These would periodically arrive in large consignments at the Barth railroad station. A truck was sent to collect them with a small party of POWs to do the loading under guard. The building that served as the parcel store was in the Vorlager, where the parcels were stored and then censored. A team of POWs were assembled in the parcel store to sort packages for the different compounds and then to open each for examination by the German censors. Any food cans were always punctured at one end to ensure the contents would be quickly consumed and not kept for escape purposes. Cigarette and tobacco packets were exposed but only occasionally did a censor examine one. All books were taken away and, if approved, later issued to the POW library. Games and clothing parcels were untied by the prisoners before being passed along a table for the censor's examination, after which they were retied and put in sacks for distribution.

Coded messages in letters told us well in advance the names of individuals to whom forbidden material was being sent, and the POW sorters were briefed on these. An aid to identification was that the packages with secret enclosures were always postmarked Alabama. When a sorter saw an Alabama postmark he alerted other POW sorters to distract the censor's attention while the special parcel was diverted to a sack of already censored parcels.

Some of the material sent was so cleverly and securely concealed that it was allowed to pass before the German censors without prior interception. Double-skin tins were a common method of getting maps, money, film, and thin items to us. Hollow spools of thread, the handles of table tennis paddles, and like objects contained the more bulky contraband such as radio tubes and camera parts.

The sleight of hand of a conjurer was developed by some of the sorters in diverting the parcels they recognized as containing forbidden items. If any had been apprehended the punishment would have been severe. Happily, it remained an unknown.

The censoring of mail both into and out of the camp was done by German interpreters at Stalag Luft III, Sagan. Coded messages were suspected and anything that looked ambiguous was blacked out—or anything not understood was regarded as suspicious. They also checked for the use of invisible ink. As far as is known they never discovered any of the many forms of coded messages that passed between POWs and the British and American agencies involved. In case they should be shot down and made prisoner, selected members of Allied air crews were taught codes to be used in correspondence with next of kin. When any of these men were notified as POWs, their letters home were intercepted and decoded. Letters containing coded messages were drafted by the intelligence people in the States or Britain to send to these POWs, who passed the information to compound security officers. The messages sent from the camp were mostly concerned with intelligence obtained from new POWs that was believed to be important in aiding the Allied cause.

Successfully hiding forbidden articles and material from our captors was always difficult and again there were some ingenious solutions. A considerable library of books had been built up over the months for POW use and it was within the covers and bindings of selected volumes that forged documents, German bank notes, maps, etc. were concealed. Only a very few people knew of this and the majority of POW readers enjoyed these books without knowing the secrets they held.

Much of the more bulky contraband could only be buried for safety. Some was deposited in the compound vegetable gardens that we were allowed. The planting and removal of a forbidden article could then be done without arousing the suspicions of any German onlookers.

There was also the risk of prisoners being discovered while about some secret task, particularly as four English-speaking "ferrets" were usually to be found in each compound during daylight hours. In addition to the POW compound security officers, every barrack building had its own security officer who was responsible for appointing and deploying "watchers" whose task it was to give warning by prearranged signals of the approach of any Germans to an area where clandestine activities were in progress. In this way the workers were not taken by surprise and had hidden incriminating evidence by the time the ferret or guard appeared. Often the appointed watchers had no idea of the nature of the secret activities they were guarding. Every party of POWs assigned to work duties in the Vorlager had its watchers. They were often able to detect any preparations for a barrack search and signal a general warning.

Yet another aspect of securing our subversive pursuits was the precautions taken to see that the Abwehr did not plant a spy in our midst. We realized that it would not be difficult for an enemy agent fluent in English to assume the identity of a dead airman and enter our society in the guise of a new prisoner. To guard against this each compound security officer had a panel who interviewed each newcomer. The questioning was thorough and it was felt good enough to trap any impostors. As far as I am aware none were ever found, and as our security was never compromised it is to be assumed no attempt was ever made to plant an informant.

The Provisional Wing X intelligence section also conducted interrogations of every new prisoner who arrived in camp, assuming that each had seen or heard something during his capture and journey to Barth that could prove useful, not least to matters that might have direct or indirect bearing on our well-being and escape efforts.

The Abwehr were no fools and knew there was some organization within the camp that fostered escapees and engaged in other clandestine activities. Counteraction consisted for the most part of having a few of their men constantly poking around the compounds to report on anything they thought might be covert. Perhaps the most aggravating functions they performed were direct ferret operations: arriving in the middle of the night to drive everyone into the sports plaza, then search a barracks from end to end looking for escape or other *verboten* equipment, slashing mattresses, tearing stoves out, chopping holes in the walls, upending lockers, looking through Red Cross parcels, and often confiscating personal articles. It appeared that they operated separately and distinctly from the Luftwaffe Kommandant's organization. Major von Miller never appeared to respond to a directive of Oberst von Warnstedt, which suggested his group worked directly from some other source, such as the SS Polizei. By virtue of his actions and those of his thugs, von Miller's presence became the most despised. There was no doubt in my mind that if he ever appeared in a compound or barracks without being surrounded by pistol-carrying guards his throat would have been cut from ear to ear.

In countenance Major von Miller, blond and tall, appeared to be about 40 years old. Having worked as an airline sales representative in the United States before the war, he had an excellent command of English. An interesting insight into his personality was that whenever a prisoner spoke to him he always answered in German. Only when he was very angry did he lapse into English. Von Miller was seldom seen to smile; I believe he may have had some sadistic sense of humor but to us he was the archetypal brutal Nazi. Even his subordinates trod lightly in his presence, no doubt for fear that to earn his displeasure might mean a trip to the Russian front. My direct contact with this officer was not often. There was no compromise in anything we discussed. His method of maintaining law and order relied on instilling fear, perhaps the oldest of man's weapons. The only way I found to oppose him was to give no evidence of fear and, fortunately for all of us, von Miller did not command the camp.

The fear that at some future date the prisoners might have to defend themselves had caused Provisional Wing X to form a secret commando squad. Primitive weapons had been made for their use and these lay buried with only a few people knowing the locations. The cudgels, knives, and knuckle-dusters were to be used to seize guns from the guards. In my view the situation would have to be very desperate indeed to resort to such measures with this pathetic armory. There was the risk too that anyone caught fashioning or in possession of a weapon might suffer a fate worse than a prolonged stay in the cooler.

The cooler was the kriegies' name for the *Stubenarrest* building where those judged guilty of some gross offense in our captor's eyes were placed in solitary confinement. For some misdemeanors, such as removing metal or wood fixtures to fashion escape tools, this could be a week; for attempts to escape, two or four weeks, although the sentence appears to have been at the whim of the prosecutors. Apart from being incarcerated in a small cell, prisoners were not allowed any Red Cross food or comforts and there was a restriction on smoking. I was informed that the punishments were becoming progressively more severe and that one recaptured US major was denied food and water until he divulged his method of escape. Thereafter he remained in solitary for much longer than was normal for his escapade.

In early January we received word that the moustached Colonel Russ Spicer, former North 2 compound commander who had been taken for trial elsewhere on the pretext of inciting prisoners to riot, was back in Stalag Luft I languishing in the cooler. As it appeared he was in for a long stay we asked permission of the Kommandant to send him a guitar, but this was refused. The harsh treatment of the prisoners appeared to increase as the fortunes of the Third Reich waned. What lay in store when the Nazi regime crumbled was not pleasant to speculate. We knew the end would witness wild and wooly days until law and order was restored.

5

Starvation Prospects

By the end of January 1945 it was evident that the combination of winter weather and insufficient food was beginning to take its toll on the POWs. Fewer people were to be seen outside. It was not just that the mud and slush surrounding the barracks blocks were no place to wander when it wasn't freezing, but rather that energies were subdued by chill and hunger. Because few Red Cross parcels were coming through, we had been forced to ration each man to a half pack a week. This further aggravated the fact that the German ration often faltered and some of the vegetables supplied were found to be frozen or rotten. To make matters worse, new prisoners were still being committed to the camp to make further inroads into the ration until the Germans saw fit to increase it.

Provisional Wing X complained, protested, and suggested; Hubbard and Zahn kept the typewriter busy with our requests to the administration. For my part the endeavor was to try and obtain some relief for my fellow prisoners through the weekly meetings with the Kommandant. And by now I had a good enough understanding of the people I was dealing with to try a ploy or two of my own. In the first place I had learned to address my questions only to von Warnstedt and not to any of the half dozen or so members of his staff who were usually present. Although he was perhaps 20 years my senior we were both full colonels, and thus I asserted my rank. If one of his minions asked me a question I purposely delayed my answer and spoke deliberately slowly to the colonel. The staff would often take several minutes to discuss the simplest point, back and forth, but I had learned not to interject. In this way formality prevailed and, I hoped, a growing acknowledgment of my command.

On the other hand, while facing up to von Warnstedt and his staff, there was no point in antagonizing them unnecessarily. On the contrary, if I was to wrest changes in their penalizing regulations, it would be through being seen to instill order in the prisoners. To this end in late January we published orders that, ostensibly, underlined my efforts to promote Wing X authority. A first move was to require prisoners to display rank and grade on clothing. This took a sizable effort and brought more than a few moans from those who could not recognize the necessity and aim. Snips of metal were cut for officers' bars and strips of rag sewn into chevrons for enlisted men. Some leaf insignia for majors and lieutenant colonels was molded out of can solder. In my case, using white string, "eagles" were laboriously hand-embroidered on my shirt collar and jacket.

I also issued an order on saluting and that this military courtesy should be observed with German officers. Here again this did my standing little good with men embittered with hatred for the enemy, who felt they were being asked to fraternize. All this was in published orders that I knew the Germans would see. In line with the Senior British Officer's decree in the West compound, on 1 February I issued a supposedly hush-hush order that all escape attempts were to be halted, making sure it was leaked to the Germans. Again this did not meet with universal approval, for prisoners did not know the ulterior motive. The truth was that Pinky

McCollom and his Saints were still to entertain support for any escape enterprise that had a chance of making it. But for the time being their efforts would far better be expended on other activities, in particular the cultivating of "friendly" guards as sources for obtaining materials, equipment, and information.

Because of the increasing shortages of certain products in Germany, the contents of a Red Cross parcel became a highly prized black market commodity outside the camp. While trading with prisoners constituted a major breach of the German military code and ethics, the open exchange of cigarettes, chocolate, and powdered coffee had been going on for months. Individual prisoners had struck their own bargains, although monitored by compound security officers, but I now felt that with food becoming desperately short we had to put more order into this situation too. Trading nourishing chocolate for a bottle of schnapps did not make much sense. However, a total stop could not be ordered as this might expose the work of McCollom's people. Long before my arrival, traders had been set up in each compound to obtain materials for our covert operations, lead, zinc, ink, rubber, and other materials to manufacture special equipment. Reichmarks, maps, and other items also had to be procured. But the most important requirement that had priority over everything else was dry cell batteries for the secret radios. Now, when all but the most indoctrinated of Nazi followers must have seen the looming defeat, we could seek more sophisticated and sinister items, namely firearms and ammunition. It is a fact of life that in any nation there are always individuals who will sell their souls for money or other entice-ment.

The trading was made easier by the type of guard that now watched us. At one time the Luftwaffe guards were young, well trained, and disciplined. As the losses on various fronts dug deeper and deeper into the limited manpower and resources of the Third Reich, the standard both militarily and intellectually dropped proportionately. Now the av-erage guard was middle-aged or had physical disabilities. Many had scant training and little indoctrination; only a military uniform differen-tiated them from civilian status. While a few of these men could be corrupted, others displayed an attitude of hatred toward the prisoners. The average guard interpreted the camp regulations as he saw fit, and any personal suffering by his family or friends was apt to spark a desire to exact revenge. This mood was further aggravated by Doctor Goebbels's propaganda, which pictured the mounting destruction of German cities and their populations as being conducted by criminals and terror fliers. Fed by this continual diet of atrocities, the hatred toward the POWs was evident in several incidents.

If, on the other hand, a trader identified a guard who showed signs of a considerable loss of faith in the Nazi cause, the man came in for special targeting. We were aware that the chief fear of most Germans was what their propaganda called "the Russian menace," the advance of the eastern hordes, barbarians who would show little mercy. If the target contact was particularly concerned about his fate when the Soviets arrived, the trader would show him the Safe Conduct Pass. This had wording in both English and German stating that the bearer had assisted POWs and should be given safe conduct. There was a space for a photo to be affixed and the card had a British Air Ministry seal. The target contact was told that when the time came he would receive one of these passes if he provided the items required. The promise usually did the trick and, with cigarettes in payment for every order honored, the man became a regular contact the trader could usually manipulate with ease. The Safe Conduct Pass was really bogus, just a clever piece of work by our forgers. Just one or two were produced and only promised, never given, to a German.

Although there was no love lost between Luftwaffe officers and the Allied POWs, I recall no instances of malicious treatment at their hands. For the most part these officers conducted themselves properly and seemed to be looking for a quiet life. We came most into contact with the Lager officers who with a small staff administered each compound. They rarely made a decision on their own, taking matters raised to the Kommandant's office and on return feigning frustration in that they could not give us an answer—although I came to believe their disenchantment with the hierarchy was genuine.

Of Lager officers known to me, perhaps the best were Major Stein-hower of North 1 and Hauptmann von Beck of West. Both possessed a rational approach to life, were well educated and not obsessed with the fanaticism of Nazi superiority. Steinhower had been a professor in math-ematics and history in a higher educational establishment prior to being drafted into Luftwaffe uniform. Well along in years, this mild-mannered ex-teacher would have much preferred to be back in his seminary writing European history rather than involved in the thankless task of trying to resolve the endless problems and complaints of a POW compound. Being fluent in English and of reasonably open mind, he could be talked to and reasoned with. Daily he'd report to the room of the "unholy four" in North 1 to partake of a cup of ersatz tea and discuss any subject. In due course I could see that Greening, McCollom, and Hubbard were in-fluencing and using this man for the POWs' best interests. That said, Steinhower was anything but a dumb stooge: he well knew his paychecks came from the Third Reich. On the other hand I doubt if he condoned negative attitudes and deprivations as dealt out by those with the real power in the Stalag Luft I administration. Much credit could be given to his efforts in assisting the establishment of theatrical plays, POW band performances, a library, educational courses, and sundry projects. From my observation, this officer was way out of place in the military.

In contrast, Hauptmann von Beck, an Austrian with World War I service, was very much the military man. This was reflected in his char-acter, straight and decisive. He knew his regulations and limitations and did not vacillate. Like all senior Lager officers he had a good command of English and was quite willing to converse on most topics. While I never did ascertain the truth, it was rumored that he had earned the dis-pleasure of his superiors in a former command and been relegated to the lowly position he now occupied. His wisdom and judgment provided ample evidence that von Beck did not approve of the continual harass-ment of his POW charges. It was obvious that he did not exist easily with the arrogant camp authority, although in earlier days he had—so I learned—been more willing to accept their policy.

The Lager officers for North 2 and 3, Hauptmanns Bloom and Probst, were less influential and more cautioned in their contact with POWs. I had little to do with them.

There were signs that the message we were trying to put over to the Kommandant was getting through—that Provisional Wing X was intent on order among the prisoners and could effect it. Von Warnstedt, and Jäger his number two, seemed more receptive to my requests for meetings and to the points raised in them. Even so, I was now more than ever convinced that dictates were coming from some other outside authority than the OKW—most likely the feared Reichsführer-SS Heinrich Himmler. Proposals that the Kommandant initially seemed to consider favorably were ultimately squashed. With the bitter weather and difficulty in keeping warm, one of my staff had raised the idea of asking the Germans if they would allow small POW parties under guard to forage for fallen branches in the surrounding pine woods. After the usual few days for the administration to digest the proposal we were delighted to hear it was approved. On 7 February our team assembled ready to leave the gate, when we were notified that the permission was canceled. The excuse was that the woods were private property but I felt there was more to this; it smacked of the policy pursued by von Miller of allowing hope to build up, then dashing it down.

Shortly after this disappointment an incident occurred that I felt could be exploited to our advantage. Broken glass was found in two of the loaves of black bread supplied from civilian bakeries for the POWs. An immediate note of complaint was put in suggesting this was the work of some fanatic taking out a grudge on the prisoners. On the same date another paper was submitted requesting that I be issued a pass to move between the four compounds during the day, without guard, on my given parole not to escape. It was pointed out that as Senior Allied Officer I was expected to know about and deal with problems in other compounds. In this connection I found it impossible to carry out German orders in writing or in the short escorted visits that had to be specially arranged. For several weeks the benefits of a pass in dealing with problems in other compounds had been put to the Lager officers and members of the Kommandant's staff who lent an ear. Hoping that some had been suitably persuaded that my ability to move at will between compounds would better help instill order, I felt it was time to make an official request while there was some embarrassment over the bread incident. A conference next day with the Kommandant's staff on a number of matters was another opportunity to push the point. Von Warnstedt was absent and I knew Jäger would defer.

I was beginning to think the pass request had ended up in the disapproved tray, but nine days after my letter, on 19 February, the *Ausweis* (pass) was granted. Hitherto doctors and chaplains were the only people to have been issued such passes. The privilege had only been extended to me because I appeared to be in sympathy with some aspects of the running of the camp. Of course, the main satisfaction was that I could now more easily communicate with the Allied commanders in the other compounds, and through two-way discussion effect real improvement in establishing policy that would strengthen Provisional Wing X and the whole POW organization in the camp.

With the Ausweis came two white arm bands to be worn when walking between compounds; its first use, to visit Gabreski in North 3, was taken with a little apprehension. Hopefully all guards had received and understood instructions regarding my passage along the area between the compounds and the outer fence, for I could not help noticing that machine guns in the guard towers followed my progress. No doubt intrigued by the sight of a lone prisoner slowly walking along outside the wire, a bunch of kriegies started cheering. This was much to my discomfort in case some trigger-happy guard thought I had pulled an escape. Few knew or recognized me, but in short order everyone, both Germans and POWs, became familiar with my daily travels from compound to compound.

Not long after its issue the Ausweis placed me in another compound at an opportune moment. One afternoon I decided to visit Cy Wilson, the commander of North 2. Soon after my arrival a commotion was seen outside one building where a number of POWs had congregated. Cy and I walked up to the scene to ask what the trouble was and were informed "a goon raid." By coincidence an Abwehr search party had entered North 2 and was in the midst of swarming through the rooms searching for any suspicious items. Crusty and indifferent as Cy usually was, he said, somewhat to my surprise, "Hub, let's go in and see what's going on." We both strode into the corridor as if we owned the place.

Von Miller seldom accompanied his 20 or so armed goons, usually delegating command to one of his subordinates. On this occasion it turned out to be Hauptmann Rath, a sleazy type, also held in disdain by the POWs, although he did not possess the shrewd, cruel mind of von Miller. Rath was taken aback by the sudden presence of two senior Allied officers. His first response was "What are you doing here?" To this I replied, "I want to see how your troops search." Perhaps this temporarily baffled him, for he threw open the nearest door saying, "Good, take a look in here." Three Abwehr henchmen were industriously going through the personal belongings of some unfortunate. The timing couldn't have been better, for one thug was just stuffing a packet of cigarettes inside his greatcoat at that moment. Normally items confiscated were carried from the barracks in open boxes; this fellow was stealing for himself. Our protestations prompted Rath to ask the man what he had put in his coat—as if he didn't already know! With great effort the befuddled guard removed the coat and handed it to the Abwehr captain. Searching through the pockets produced three packets of American cigarettes. Although embarrassed, Rath soon regained his composure and informed us we had no right in the building while it was being searched. But the truth was out; we had long complained about the pilfering that took place under the guise of a security search, always to have the administration indignantly refute this slander on German honor. Now we had caught one red-handed and in full view of his own officer. We demanded the name of the guilty soldier. Rath refused, but he clearly smarted under the embarrassment and immediately stopped the search, withdrawing his men from the compound.

Stealing was not solely the prerogative of our enemies. To supply our various secret enterprises, theft had long been an organized business. Tools, uniforms, and various materials were stolen from workmen and

The Hub: Colonel Hubert Zemke. A photograph taken while I was commanding the 56th Fighter Group in England.

About to climb into the cockpit of my P-51 Mustang at Wattisham air base, a few days before I went down over Germany.

Contrasting vertical views of Stalag Luft I, taken April and November 1944 and illustrating the extent of the camp's enlargement during the intervening period.

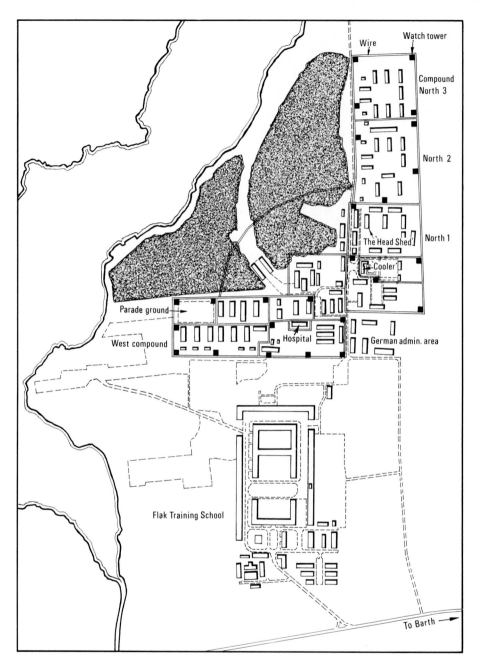

Annotated plan of Stalag Luft I as of January 1945.

Morning Appell in West compound sports area. The spire of Barth cathedral can be seen on the horizon.

One of 25 wooden guard towers situated outside the compound fences. Spotlights were used by guards to search shadowed areas of buildings.

The double barbed wire fence that surrounded the camp and separated each compound. Coils of barbed wire filled the space between the fences to deter crawl-through escapees.

The "cooler," the solitary confinement block in the Vorlager where POW offenders served their sentences on bread and water. Note the angled window shuttering which only allowed occupants a view of the sky.

Luftwaffe guard at the gate leading to
North 1 compound.

Oberst Scherer, Luftwaffe commander of
Stalag Luft I when I arrived. A first-rate
authoritarian, his indifference caused
us continual anguish and harassment.
Fortunately he was replaced early in 1945.

Lt. Col. C. Ross Greening was a highly
talented individual and could turn his hand
to a variety of skills. A gifted artist, he
executed this self-portrait while in captivity.

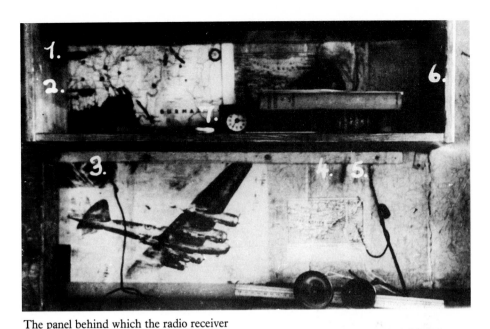

The panel behind which the radio receiver and batteries were hidden. The photographs and maps cut from magazines served as camouflage. (1) and (2) Screwdrivers in position for working the tuning controls. When not in use the screwdrivers were removed from the holes though the panels and replaced by small plugs disguised as the black spots of towns on the map. (3) The aerial clipped to a nail which was connected through the panel to the radio. (4) and (5) Two other nails used as connections for earphone leads. (6) The nails were part of a row that appeared to be used to secure the bookshelf above. (7) The alarm clock to awaken the operators.

The panel hinged open to reveal the radio receiver. Wires led to 50–60 flashlight batteries coupled together to provide power for the set.

A forged camp pass. It appears to have been
printed but it was actually all done by hand.

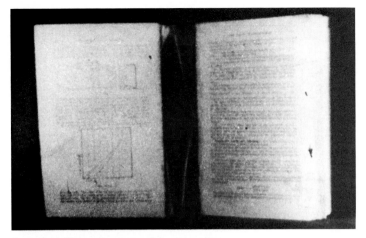

One of the library books used for concealing documents. The page binding was cut and the cover boards split open to take the material to be hidden. If the work was done carefully, when glued together again it was impossible to tell the book had been tampered with. Many books were used for this purpose, and this method of concealment was never discovered.

Morning attention to personal hygiene in the wash shed. Only cold water ran from the spigots and was close to freezing in winter.

POWs unloading potatoes under the watchful eye of a guard. Deliveries received during the winter of 1944–45 were nearly always second grade and often many had started to decay.

The life-enhancing Red Cross food parcels being unloaded by prisoners at the central store. These parcels were allotted to compounds by the number of POWs in each.

The ration of brickets—made from coal dust—arrived by horse-drawn transport. The same wagons served just about all our transport around the camp, even as makeshift hearses.

A religious service in West compound. This building also served as a theater—and, unknown to all but a select few, as the hiding place for one of our radios. The pews shown here were built of Red Cross parcel crating.

SONDER-

Ausweis

für den

S.A.O. Oberst Hubert Zemke

Dieser Ausweis berechtigt den durch Lichtbild ausgewiesenen Inhaber, zwischen dem Morgen-und Nachmittag- Zählappell ohne deutsche Begleitung sämtliche Teillager zu betreten.

Barth, den 15.2.45.

gez. Schroeder

Hptm. u. A.O.

Unterschrift des Kgf.

Zemke's Ausweis. A photograph taken after my capture, the swollen face making me look every bit the "Terrorflieger." The Ausweis was of great value, allowing me to visit all prisoner compounds of Stalag Luft I. My sworn parole was given that I would not attempt to escape by using this document.

Among the long-time British army prisoners was Captain M. A. Charton, who was the chaplain for Catholic services.

After the mess hall in North 1 was destroyed by fire, the German authorities issued mobile field kitchens to enable one meal of the day to be prepared. About to ladle out the day's offering is Lieutenant John C. Morgan. "Red" Morgan was the only flier in captivity who had won the Medal of Honor. Prior to my arrival he had achieved fame for distilling an alcoholic morale-raiser from food parcel raisins.

The volunteer POW drivers and the two trucks provided through the Swedish Red Cross to transport food parcels from Lübeck. The drivers were put on parole not to escape, although Luftwaffe guards rode with them. The trucks were painted white with red crosses on roofs in the hope that they would escape Allied air attack.

A view of the library in the German part of the camp. Unbeknown to our captors, many of these books concealed our forged documents, German banknotes, and other secret material.

buildings in the Vorlager whenever the opportunity arose. With the usual distraction of attendant Germans by one prisoner, another removed the required item. Not all attempts were successful, and if caught the thief was quickly jailed in the cooler.

Sadly, thieving was not confined to the enemy's property. It was at this time that Gabby reported a growing incidence of stealing in North 3. Even though a high state of camaraderie and a "sink or swim together" attitude prevailed among most POWs, we had our bad eggs who would pilfer food and cigarettes from others. These cases were comparatively few in a camp of thousands, but if the culprits were apprehended they were dealt with severely. When people were near starving this became an even more heinous crime. During February Gabby reported a rash of thefts and quarrels in North 3. The trouble involved a band of enlisted men who had been evacuated from a Stalag at Heidi in Poland as the Soviet armies moved inexorably westward. Mostly sergeant air gunners, these people were a piteous sight when they arrived frost-bitten, exhausted, and half-starved. Our privations were as nothing compared with what they had endured. From interrogation we soon established that there had been no cohesive organization in their old camp to proclaim their rights and resist indignities forced on them by the German authorities.

Once these newcomers' health had improved it was noticed that two of their number tended to dominate the rest. These ringleaders were an Italian-American named Angione who, it was discovered, had a prison record in the States, and another sergeant, of Irish background, called O'Day. After a number of unpleasant incidents matters came to a head with a raid on the new mess hall constructed between North 2 and North 3. Angione and O'Day were apprehended stealing food, duly chastised, and reduced to the rank of private. Notwithstanding this, O'Day defied the recognized authority of Gabby's staff, and when reasoned with swore and struck out before being physically restrained. Even then he attacked his guards with a knife. Both men were recommended for courts martial and, surprisingly, von Warnstedt approved my request to have them jailed for a period of solitary in his cooler without asking for justification. When the men were returned to the compound I went to see them. The cooler had mellowed their arrogance but they refused to recognize my authority. When Angione threatened to reveal to the Germans that the POWs had an underground news service and certain details of our clandestine activities he had heard about, the interview ended. They were told in no uncertain terms what the fate of collaborators would be. From that day two POW guards were assigned to stay with these men wherever they went—even to the latrine. If either attempted to talk to the Germans, these guards had instructions what to do to silence them. We had no more trouble.

The critical food situation increased the temptation to steal, but apart from the case of Angione and O'Day there were few instances. From my travels around the compounds it was obvious that men were losing weight and vigor: in other words they were slowly starving. Having already cut the rations supplied by 12 percent, the Germans were forced to reduce them still further. While I suspected their policy held that the best way to subdue a man was to keep his stomach half-empty, there was no doubt the reserves of food in the Reich were under strain. Our guards may have been able to eat their fill, but the actual food was little better than ours in scope and palatability. The meager and halting flow of Red Cross parcels from Switzerland now restricted each prisoner to a quarter pack per week. Allied air attacks were offered as the chief reason and this was probably true.

As if the depredations we already suffered were not enough, the administration received orders to limit the amount of clothing each prisoner possessed; and this while we were still having to contend with snow, ice, and the freezing easterlies that swept the camp. We fought back verbally as best we could, and with letters again beseeched the Swiss Protecting Power to come to our aid, but to little avail. The prisoners were poorly attired for winter by any standard and could ill afford to part with any garment.

Most, like myself, had a peculiar mixture of uniform, patched, darned, and modified. There were exceptions; three people in particular amazed me with how smart they remained. Einar Malstrom, the six-foot commander of the US detachment in West compound, in his dark olive officer's trousers and tunic with full insignia stood out like a beacon among the rest of us. There was always a crease in those pants. I once chided him that he must have a contact who took them for dry cleaning. With a pointed sweep of his eyes over Zemke's stained and worn garb, plus a perky touch of sarcasm, he retorted that he thought a commanding officer's duty was to maintain the dignity of his rank and be prepared to go down in full military attire. The second of these natty dressers was Group Captain Cecil Weir, the Senior British Officer since the beginning of the year and a man with whom I had established a good rapport. Ginger Weir, who escaped from a crippled Lancaster in December, obviously had full uniform under a flying suit on that last mission. He appeared in camp as if he had just been outfitted in Saville Row, London. However, the most immaculately dressed man in the camp was, in my opinion, Lieutenant Colonel George Hankey, the British Army doctor who ran our hospital. Always sharp in appearance, with trim moustache and haircut, he was to be seen in a splendid British greatcoat and officer's peaked cap. The parade ground appearance belied the dedication and industry of this man, who had little opportunity to rest from tending the camp sick. Doc Hankey had the advantage over most of us in that he had not arrived in prison camp via a parachute, although we did not envy him for being in his fifth year of confinement. Captured at Dunkirk in 1940, he had prevailed upon his German counterparts to allow his footlocker to go with him to various POW camps in the years that followed. At least our captors were reasonably benevolent to the medical people.

An outcome of the limitations on clothing was that when the temperature dropped to zero we were disinclined to do any laundry. Having nothing else to wear meant one had to stand around for hours wrapped in nothing but a blanket waiting for garments to dry out. In due time the reluctance to launder brought an aroma of tuned-up billy goat permeating through one's clothing. This condition, understandably, quickly brought complaints and threats from roommates so that a trip to the mess hall to get a bucket of hot water could be delayed no longer.

The camp administrators paid only lip service to POW cleanliness, for they could not enforce much of anything with the skimpiest issues of soap, cleaning rags, mops, and brushes. In fact we had to make our own primitive brooms and scrub brushes in camp to combat the mud deposited by boots on barrack floors.

Aside from personal hygiene, shaving presented a challenge as the regular issue of blades to every POW was simply out of the question. In my case an evening ritual resulted. While engaging in a skull session with the three lieutenant colonels or quietly reflecting on the past day's events and what could be capitalized on, the cutting edges of my solitary double-edged blade were gradually restored. By the light of a flickering candle the blade was carefully stroked back and forth with one finger against the inner side of a cheap drinking glass. Not the best of hones but, with time of little importance, perseverance could result in reasonably good restoration. The blade needed to be sharp as most shaves were without lather on the stubble.

Butcher haircuts were the desired style as this helped the fight against body lice. Clippers and scissors had been supplied by the Germans for this task but, as with most things, far too few for the job. In North 1 a kriegie managed a haircut about once every six weeks. For the occupants of room 21, Greening usually played barber, accepting the task as a challenge to his inherent artistic talent.

Although prisoners were forbidden to have money, Provisional Wing X did have the means to purchase articles and commodities from the Germans. German POWs in the USA were permitted three dollars a week—paid by the US government—with which to purchase personal requisites. On a reciprocal basis the Germans agreed to similar purchasing power being available to each of their American prisoners. However, our attempts to make purchases of permitted items—such as razor blades—were regularly turned down on the pretext that the items were not available. Admittedly the German economy was under severe strain at this date and much was in short supply. Even so it became plain to us that the refusals were based either on a fear that the material requested would be used for escape and other covert purposes, or on the general policy of POW suppression. Nevertheless Provisional Wing X kept accounts that totaled the amount of dollars in this fund. The growing purchasing power of the prisoners became an acute embarrassment to the German administration, who attempted to diminish it by frequent deductions for the cost of repair and damage which they insisted was caused by prisoners in the camp. Provisional Wing X staff held that much of this was due to normal wear and tear and contested the claims. Even with these appropriations from the fund it still grew at a considerable rate.

March came and still winter held grip on Stalag Luft I, if less severely than in past weeks. Neither was there relief in our serious food situation. Red Cross parcel wagons dispatched from Switzerland disappeared on the mutilated railroad system of the Reich and there was no improvement in the pitiful German rations. On the current 800 to 1,000 calories a day per prisoner it didn't need a medical authority to predict that the prison population would be reduced to skin and bone in a month or so. The kriegies were noticeably more subdued and food was now more than ever the most frequent topic of conversation. The supply of Red Cross parcels dried up completely and the German ration further deteriorated. Toward the end of the month some men were so weak they couldn't stand when first getting off their beds in the morning. A few others were caught picking over the garbage cans for scraps and it became necessary to post our own guards to prevent this. We had enough problems without people eating waste that would undoubtedly make them sick.

Then by a quirk of fate our trusty medical chief, Lieutenant Colonel Hankey, received an invitation to attend a meeting with the German medical authorities in Berlin on health problems in prison camps. This came as a most surprising development to say the least, considering the attitudes of OKW and the local German authorities. The surprise was not that the German medical people had convened such a meeting—for those who truly minister to the sick and wounded are not bound by national, religious, or political restraints—but that they had been allowed to do so by the totalitarian regime. Hankey was well aware of the malnutrition in the camp and needed no encouragement from me or others to make known our situation to the people of influence with whom he would surely come into contact. We were not without hope that the good Doc might be able to obtain us some relief.

An idea proposed before my arrival in camp was revived, that the Red Cross ship parcels directly from Sweden to one of the nearby ports. If trucks were also sent we could provide prisoners on parole to get the parcels from docks to camp. Von Warnstedt did not disapprove, although he seemed anxious that his masters should not think he was advocating the move. We took every step we could to impress the seriousness of the food situation on both the German administration and the Swiss Protecting Power. In desperation we even used our secret radio transmitter to convey the measure of our plight to Allied sources.

With a body of men now swelled to more than 7,000 and existing on meager rations, it was remarkable there were few fatal medical cases. By the law of averages we could not all hope to avoid the grim reaper. On 12 March Second Lieutenant William Cassel died in the hospital of leukemia, the first prisoner to die of natural causes since my taking command. Acting immediately to set up an appropriate military funeral, I was informed by the German headquarters that there would be no American flag or wreath on the coffin, even though these were made up by prisoners. Also no sounding of taps, a final send-off to the dead in our military tradition. In fact, anything to upgrade the last military dignity to the deceased companion was turned down. Perhaps my anger at this pettiness caused them to relent a little and allow pallbearers to give a hand salute at the graveside. All the same, we resolved to carry the ceremony along with as much military bearing as possible. Fifteen pallbearers were allowed; myself and another from Wing Headquarters, Lieutenant Colonel Gabreski and a party from North 3 where Cassel had recently lived, and the remainder a British contingent led by Group Captain Weir. Probably fearful of a demonstration of support, the Germans ordered the funeral party to assemble at 0600 hours on 15 March, a time when it was still dark and the prisoners would be locked up.

The chilly morn found the burial party marching out of the camp with the bare coffin loaded on the same four-wheel horse-drawn cart that transported our coal and vegetables. Taking our slow steps to the Barth town cemetery, we in turn were escorted by ten German guards toting submachine guns. It was just growing light when the wooden casket was lowered into the grave.

Walking back to Stalag Luft I, I turned my head skyward and winked at the guy up there whoever he may be and thanked Bill Cassel. For out of his passing had come some good in that a few of us had been able to walk outside that oppressive barbed wire for the first time in many a long day. A sad thought, perhaps, but that young man was already freed from this precarious life. Unhappily, this was not the only funeral I was to attend, the next as a result of an alarming trend in our containment.

6

The Shifting Scene

When first occupied by RAF and American prisoners, Stalag Luft I had rarely been disturbed by air raid warnings. The picture had changed dramatically during recent months, and while we might rarely see or hear Allied aircraft, air raid warnings were commonplace. When these occurred all prisoners had to return to their barracks blocks and remain there until the "all clear." The problem was that with the hubbub of a camp containing thousands, warnings were not always heard. Camp regulations stated that any POW seen outside during an air raid alert was liable to be fired on by guards, and there had been instances of this. The first I had to deal with occurred one Sunday afternoon in mid-January when a prisoner in North 2 walked out of his barracks to go to the latrine. Without warning two shots rang out and bullets thudded into the ground near him. The offender had no idea an air raid alarm had been given. Nor for that matter did a church party who had earlier walked back to their barracks. A rigorous protest was made to the Kommandant but no concessions were forthcoming apart from promises of some sort of acoustic siren in future. The problem was that the whistle warnings given by the tower guards were not always heard. The situation was compounded by instructors in the adjacent flak school continually blowing whistles on training activities. Further protests on this matter resulted in the promise that guards would walk through each compound blowing whistles when a raid warning was notified.

There was no more trouble until early March when the 8th Air Force was pounding targets somewhere to the south of us. No guard made a whistle warning in North 1 and when two prisoners—both oblivious of the situation—popped out of barracks they were immediately greeted by shots. One man ran for his life into an open doorway where several POWs, on hearing the firing, had thrown themselves on the floor. The bullets passed the fleeing man to smash through the wall of the building, narrowly missing the other occupants. A protest was again registered without any results. A week later indiscriminate firing was reported in West compound during an air raid, with a bullet going through a barracks. Von Warnstedt still took no action to curb his trigger-happy guards.

Our worst fears were realized on 18 March when the 8th Air Force was in the Berlin area and a long air raid confinement took place. About 45 minutes after the alert was given at 1030 hours a South African Air Force officer in the British compound, Lieutenant G. V. Whitehouse, forgetfully left his barracks with a basin full of kitchen refuse. He was in the process of spreading this on his kitchen garden as a manure dressing when a walking guard shouted and fired at the same time. The 7.92 mm bullet, fired at about 40 yards range, passed through Whitehouse's body and two room walls in a barracks 60 yards distant. The severely wounded Whitehouse dropped in his tracks to be retrieved by friends. When finally rushed to the dispensary he was operated on immediately by Lieutenant Colonel Townsend, in charge during Hankey's absence. With the destruction of a kidney and serious internal hemorrhage, Townsend's surgery undoubtedly saved Whitehouse's life, although he was to remain a hospital case to the end of the war.

Around ten minutes later Second Lieutenant E. F. Wyman, who had been visiting friends in a barracks before the air raid alarm was given, started to walk casually back to his billet. Realizing too late that there were no other prisoners about, he turned and dashed back to the door he had just left. As he reached it a bullet struck him in the head and he fell bleeding, half in and half out of the doorway. Fellow prisoners dragged him into the hallway and did what they could. The next problem was how to get a doctor and raise the alarm. Only by beating on the walls and shouting in crescendo was the attention of a tower guard attracted to call the authorities to investigate. Twenty minutes passed before medical help arrived and with an armed guard Wyman was removed to the hospital. He was beyond medical help and died that afternoon.

These two incidents stirred the camp internees to the last man; never before had I seen such hatred expressed toward the Germans. There was a determined defiance. Not until the raid past signal in the afternoon was I allowed to proceed to the West compound and inspect the scene of these firings. Von Warnstedt had come and gone by the time of my arrival but at least it appeared that for once he had initiated his own investigation. The Luftwaffe guards who fired had been outside the compound wire and did not challenge either man before firing. In Wyman's case it must have been obvious that he was making every effort to get back in the barracks. These guards had been looking for an excuse to open fire, which reflected their bitterness toward the prisoners, conditioned as they were to believe us to be terror fliers.

A request for an audience with the Kommandant was granted for next day and that night saw a great deal of discussion in room 21 as to what should be said. This, like all meetings with the Kommandant, required a written submission of the points to be raised. Great care was taken in framing our protest in German as von Warnstedt spoke no English. I was determined that our message would not be diluted by an interpreter and that I rehearse what I intended to say to him in person.

As usual only a single aide was allowed to accompany me to take notes. We were confronted with a larger assembly of the Kommandant's staff than normal at such meetings. My strategy was carefully worked out to make these officers feel as uncomfortable as I could. Once seated in the chair facing von Warnstedt I did not take my eyes off the Kommandant's face, literally looking him straight in the eyes whenever I could. The room was quiet while the Oberst read over my protest; indeed for once his henchmen said nothing, but in any case I ignored them as if they didn't exist. Finally von Warnstedt raised his head and in a subdued tone asked, "What do you wish to say?" Intent on avoiding argument and ridicule, I simply emphasized what was in our written statement, that the camp authorities had constantly allowed breaches of the 1929 Geneva Convention for prisoners of war which Germany had signed. Unless he took a firm hand to stop such flagrant violations as had occurred yesterday there would be repercussions and violence that both parties would regret. The meeting was short, to the point, and, I hoped, disturbing for von Warnstedt and his staff.

As a result of this tragedy the Germans made a so-called concession that no guard would fire if a prisoner raised his hands. An absurdity, for how was a prisoner to know when to raise his hands unless he was first challenged. I can only conclude that the failure to impress on his guards the necessity to challenge before firing was meant to instill fear into prisoners. If any disciplinary action was taken against the guards concerned in the shootings we did not hear of it. We were still apparently targets for any guard who found an excuse to open fire. Only ten days after the killing of Wyman, two RAF sergeants were taking a late stroll round the West compound when a shot was aimed at them from the nearby German barracks. Fortunately the bullet missed.

The loathing for the Germans that followed the fatal shooting was relieved by a good deal of goon baiting. Whether one looked on it as practical joking or deliberate antagonism, it was something that Provisional Wing X ostensibly deplored. In reality we closed a blind eye to many pranks we became aware of, although usually the perpetrators made sure the Head Shed didn't get to hear until after the event. For the most part, goon baiting took the form of threats and insults to those guards who, not understanding English, were oblivious of what was actually being said. "You Nazi bastard, your corpse will soon be floating in the Baltic" might sound like a friendly salutation if said with a smile. There were certain individuals who made a hobby of goon baiting despite the likely result that they would end up with a spell in the cooler. One such was Major Fred Bronson in North 2. Bronson had spent time in the cooler before my arrival for a misdemeanor but was not deterred. On one or two occasions in January he had earned the Lager officers' displeasure by refusing to comply with the camp regulation that POWs should not have their hands in their pockets when being counted in Appell. On one cold day when Bronson told his boys to put their hands in their pockets they rejoined with, "We all want to go to the cooler." On another occasion Bronson continued his goon baiting by appearing for Appell as the sole member of his block and for ten minutes feigning inability to order his charges to parade. A further irritation for the Lager staff practiced by Bronson's men was at dismissal from roll call to turn east and all shout in unison, "Come on Joe, Come on Joe!," a chant of encouragement to the Soviet army. Then one day in February when there had been trouble with the piped water, Bronson asked the Lager staff if an emergency hole could be dug to collect water should the normal supply fail again. He was given permission but told the Lager staff would determine where the hole could be sited. Bronson's curt retort was: "Well hurry up; we have to get the hole dug so there is water when Stalin arrives." After that Bronson was off to the cooler again.

While baiting the Luftwaffe guards was a not infrequent exercise to relieve the boredom, getting one over on the Abwehr security police was another matter altogether. It was not, however, beyond POW ingenuity. It had been noticed that when a ferret operation was in progress the Abwehr personnel would bring a box containing hundreds of photographs and fingerprint documents into a compound. This allowed them more easily to identify and apprehend individuals who had forbidden items in personal belongings. Also noticed was that invariably this box would be set down just inside the entrance corridor of the building being searched. A plan was hatched to distract any ferret who might be nearby and steal the box. Despite the risk involved it was carried out successfully, bringing in its wake a full-scale search of the whole compound to unearth the stolen goods. Try as they might, the Abwehr men could not find any of the contents, despite turning the place upside down a couple of times. They seemed to believe the prisoners wanted the contents, whereas they were really of no interest at all to us. From the outset the plan had been for the contents of the box to be quickly distributed and for all recipients to make haste to their barracks stoves. While the Abwehr searched their quest was going up in flames, providing that little bit of welcome extra warmth. Pretty soon every POW in the compound was ordered onto the parade ground while a search was conducted. As they waited there several men staged a ruse by pretending to hide material by scraping up small heaps of sand with their feet. This had the ferrets scraping in the dirt.

If we could obtain little satisfaction from the Kommandant over the indiscriminate shooting by his guards, he did continue to show some cooperation in the matter of obtaining Red Cross parcels. At least someone somewhere in Germany had taken action and agreed to the Swedish Red Cross immediately shipping a sizable number of American Red Cross food parcels—already stockpiled in Sweden—to the port of Lübeck. On 26 March we received our first large delivery and two days later had our 30,000 parcels in store. Once again we could allow our people one parcel each per week. From then on supplies of food and other parcels from the Red Cross were never a real problem and our reserve stocks continued to increase. An important factor was the German acceptance of a scheme whereby trucks with fuel were supplied through the Swedish Red Cross and we provided drivers on parole to make collection runs to Lübeck or Rostock and back. Of course, it was to the Germans' advantage to cooperate because the more food from the International Red Cross, the more relief to their own marginal resources.

The trucks, painted white with Red Cross markings, kept up a fairly regular shuttle. We had no problem in getting volunteers despite the very real hazard of being strafed by Allied fighters. The Germans had two armed guards ride with each truck, and while there could have been problems given POW feelings after the recent shootings, the relationships turned out to be fairly equable. The common need to keep a constant watch on the sky superseded any festering enmity. On a couple of occasions at least they had to get the trucks off the road in a hurry when buzzing P-51s happened by, but there are no recollections that any trucks on these runs were actually strafed.

The German camp authorities' more reasoned approach to our welfare at this time was undoubtedly due to the Allies launching their spring offensive, for on 24 March British and American forces bridged the Rhine and began to fan across the German homeland. The confidence of those Germans who looked to some last-minute miracle to save the Third Reich from doom was fast eroding and daily more evident to us in many ways by late March. I had long believed that von Warnstedt, like his subordinate officers, rarely made a major policy decision affecting the POWs, instead communicating with his superiors in the OKW or Reichsführer SS for guidance. In some instances in the past the Kommandant had displayed touches of benevolence. For example the prisoners who helped the German team fight a fire in West compound early in March were awarded a two-hour walk in the surrounding countryside— with escort, of course. On other matters his intransigence was exasperating. For months we had tried to obtain permission to paint or have painted a Red Cross sign on the hospital and suitable identifying signs for POWs in both English and Russian on the roofs of our barracks. The fear that the camp might inadvertently be mistaken for a German barracks was very real, particularly with us one-time aviators who knew the difficulties of correctly identifying a target. Even now, at the end of March, this request was turned down, I suspect on the directions of his masters who would probably be only too happy to capitalize on the propaganda value of an Allied air attack on their own people, particularly if it were Soviet aircraft against a British-American camp.

But there were now signs that on some matters von Warnstedt was prepared to act without consulting higher authority. Had he wanted to consult, he would not have agreed to the use of POW drivers on the Red Cross trucks for the delayed supplies. McCollom's Saints had at this time, through the disillusionment of a certain man in the Stalag headquarters, gained knowledge of the communications that came and were sent. The subject of the Red Cross truck crews and associated matters never featured in any correspondence, suggesting the Kommandant was not looking for orders on this matter. Yet another loosening of the chains that bound us, which I also suspected was a direct action by von Warnstedt and those of his staff who had a more sympathetic attitude to the prisoners, was the lifting of the absurd directive on an individual's holdings from food parcels. Throughout March there had been a continual round of complaints and vilification over the limitations of cigarettes (one packet), soap and chocolate (six bars of each) accumulated by a prisoner at any one time. Any of these items over the stipulated number were confiscated by von Miller's Abwehr ferrets. Our argument was that the Red Cross parcels should not enhance the German economy, being a direct gift to the POWs who should be allowed to handle distribution as they saw fit. The knowledge that the Swiss Protecting Power representative was scheduled to visit the camp on 10 April also probably influenced the quashing of this restriction.

Yet another instance of a change in attitude came with the authorization of ten-man parties to go out and cut rushes in the nearby reed beds. The supply of wood shavings for mattresses had dried up in February and I had taken the suggestion to the Kommandant that rushes were close at hand and would make an excellent substitute filling. The usual vacillation took place, with the principal excuses for disapproving being that cutting tools were not available and that they might be used as weapons. My contention that we could soon make sufficient tools and that ten men armed with scythes were hardly going to attack four guards with submachine guns made no difference. Then, suddenly, the approval was given. Having obtained considerable quantities of reeds we suggested we be allowed to make floor mats and baskets, a harmless enough extension, but in another mystifying instance of administration logic the plea was turned down for security reasons.

Our masters were not so stingy in another matter, probably because they too would benefit. Since early in the year supplies of salt diminished until they were no longer forthcoming from the German sources. Our keepers had none for themselves either. This dearth was made known to the incarcerated, now some 8,000, and from that multitude arose an unknown graduate in chemistry who declared that he could make salt from sea water. By this date I had ceased to be amazed by the talent that existed in the camp and, while this claim seemed too good to be true, I was prepared to let him try. The first step was to request a small quantity of sea water for experimental purposes and a liter was provided. Our chemist first let the sea water percolate through a container of sand. He then made a filter out of toilet paper and placed it under the sand container before pouring fresh water through the sand. This left a dirty-looking scum on the filter. The taste of this residue was undoubtedly salty even if it didn't appear much like the ingredient used in cooking. Our chemist said the impurities came chiefly from seaweed. Amazed, I sent the German staff a sample and requested larger quantities of the Baltic so we could go into mass production. Equally amazed, the Germans allowed the skating rink in West compound to be flooded from the bay and also provided wooden barrels for distillation. As we currently had more toilet paper than food, filters were no problem. The only difficulty was the slowness of production. The scheme got under way in the first week of April, only to be terminated when news came that a carload of rock salt had arrived in the Barth railroad station.

This same chemist also proposed that we could secretly make black powder explosive given certain materials from outside. While the purchase of these through our tame guards was possible and explosives might be an asset if things got really nasty, McCollom's review board turned down the idea, mainly for fear that if anything went wrong in the manufacturing process a number of kriegies could be blown up. The commandos did, however, make and stockpile Molotov cocktails— gasoline-based incendiary grenades.

The matter of self-defense, however, became of increasing concern with the prospect of the Third Reich's demise and fears as to what would be the fate of Allied POWs. Rumors were rife, but we could do little more than speculate as to what the Nazi beast would do in its last throes. While we in Provisional Wing X might have some quite heated debates on the moves to make, we were unanimous in expanding training of the

commando-type force as well as those who would become military police. There was a faction who felt we should take the initiative as soon as
opportunity allowed and take over the camp by force. This I strongly
resisted, for it would only succeed with heavy loss of life and the repercussions could be horrendous; just the excuse the SS might need to carry
out mass extermination. In my view we should endeavor to take over the
camp peacefully, and to this end I felt we should begin by letting the
Luftwaffe administration know how they would be treated in the event
of our taking control. This was done by preparing and posting Provisional Wing X Post Regulations which detailed how both Allied and
enemy personnel would conform when control of the camp was transferred. Within these regulations it was stated plainly that there would be
no individual reprisals against enemy personnel. Purposely, a copy found
its way to von Warnstedt.

Surprisingly, there were no repercussions. The war was not over; the
Germans were still very much in charge of Stalag Luft I and could have
confined me and the Wing staff to the cooler for this audacious publication. Instead they chose to ignore it; the matter was not even mentioned
at the next meeting with the Kommandant. A good sign; the Luftwaffe
staff had obviously discussed the notice and decided it could be a lifeline
for them. These regulations may have been less well received by some
Allied prisoners who, understandably, could not wait to run wild. To them
the Head Shed's proclamation on military organization was anathema.

In those early days of April as the Allied drives on the western front
gathered momentum and the Soviets besieged Berlin, the changing attitude of both Luftwaffe and Abwehr personnel in the camp was evident
in several ways. Ferret raids became fewer, von Miller showed himself
less and less, and I began to draw salutes from German guards on my
wanderings through various parts of the camp. Gate guards clicking their
heels as I passed through made me smile, as a few weeks past a sullen
stare amounted to the only acknowledgment when I presented my Ausweis. Now, of course, it could be assumed that the *amerikanische Oberst*
could hold a key to their fortunes in the not too distant future.

I looked to capitalize still further on this apparent change in attitude observed in the camp administration. A visit of the representative of the Swiss Protecting Power was scheduled for 10 April and this seemed an opportune occasion to make the next bold move. As a preliminary I asked von Warnstedt if he would agree to a private meeting between the two of us with the Swiss diplomat present. To this he concurred.

In order to see that signatories to the Geneva Convention conformed to the agreement on prisoner of war rights, a designated representative of a neutral country made periodic visits to POW camps, in this case a Herr Albert Kadler who proved to have a reasonable command of English. Tall and fortyish, he struck me as having a rational perspective while taking a very neutral line on all issues. True, he had no authority to issue orders, but it was soon apparent that he was too much of a diplomat. Prior to the meeting we had prepared a long agenda listing the many matters we wished to raise, depositing this, as required, with the camp authorities. These points were raised one by one at the meeting and Kadler listened hard and long, taking copious notes. At least, I thought, what we said would be passed on to the Western Allies despite his circumspect attitude.

Following a tour of Stalag Luft I compounds, Kadler spent a long afternoon with the Kommandant in his office. Just what transpired between the two was never known, but as few changes were introduced after Kadler's departure it seems unlikely he was arguing our causes.

When Herr Kadler and von Warnstedt emerged I was summoned to join them. "You wanted to speak in private?" the Kommandant asked. "Yes," I replied. "Then we will go for a walk," he responded. With instructions to the guards the gates were opened and I found myself for the first time since coming to Stalag Luft I walking free without an armed guard. From this development I concluded that von Warnstedt did not want to use his inner office to be sure we were not overheard. This in itself suggested he had some inkling of what I might say.

Once the three of us were well outside the main gate I opened the conversation by saying the war was nearing its end and to save lives on both sides a plan should be quickly drawn up to transfer Stalag Luft I from the German administration to that of Provisional Wing X. I made it plain that in such circumstances no revenge would be exacted on the German authority. If the Kommandant entertained the proposal would he, Kadler, in the neutral role assist both parties in drawing up such plans? Before von Warnstedt could respond, the hitherto calm and collected Kadler exploded into protest. More accurately, he seemed to panic and shouted he could have no part in such a scheme. In short, the gist of his outburst was that the Protecting Power could not participate in agreements between protagonists as it would infringe its neutrality. More likely Kadler was afraid of blighting his own diplomatic career by unauthorized initiative. From his excited state it was quite plain that the attempt to enlist him as an arbitrator had come to nothing. Turning to von Warnstedt I said, "It appears there is no purpose in continuing this meeting." All the way back to camp Herr Kadler excitedly rattled on about why this was outside his jurisdiction. His words were wasted, for I was in no mood or position to argue. The gamble had failed. There was, however, one consolation in that von Warnstedt had made no comment on my proposal nor shown any anger. To me this meant that it was an option he might yet consider. Many years later I was able to read the report of his visit that Kadler had submitted to both the Allied and German authorities. Absolutely nothing was recorded of my proposal. Even at this stage of the war, when Germany's collapse was obviously imminent, Kadler was still playing it right down the middle.

The first signs of spring, the increase in food, and the prospect of Allied victory close at hand did wonders for the morale and general wellbeing of Stalag Luft I inmates. The post-Appell chorus of "Come on Joe" to the east and "Come on Ike" to the west became a regular feature, now ignored by the guards. We were seeing more outlandish goon baiting, and while I should have frowned on the three perpetrators of one incident, like everyone else in the camp, I could not suppress a chuckle. At afternoon Appell one of the squadrons in North 1 was drawn to attention. The Lager staff stopped dead in their tracks with amazement. Before them in the front row stood a decapitated prisoner with only a bloody pulp projecting from his greatcoat and a pop-eyed naked head under each arm. The headless wonder was a prisoner who had hunched himself up inside an oversize coat and placed a piece of bad horsemeat, rejected by the cookhouse, on top of his head. His two fellow conspirators, having shaved off all hair and added some cosmetic effect, crept up directly behind the decapitated figure, pushing their heads under his looped arms. The three men were quickly taken from the ranks and marched off to the cooler to the cheers of other prisoners on the parade ground. Only men with high morale would attempt such a prank, knowing very well what the far from pleasant punishment would be.

Such acts may have allowed bored individuals to let off steam and give their comrades a laugh, but were little more than an annoyance to the German administration. There were occasional opportunities when something could be organized that was almost certain to have a psychological effect on our wardens. The night of 12 April brought news from the BBC via our secret radios that President Roosevelt had died. The word was passed to me when the barracks were unlocked next morning. Later, after consultation with my staff, an instruction went out by word of mouth that all American POWs would wear a black armband as a sign of mourning. By cutting up strips of black rag—or the expedient of soot or boot polish on a lighter color—a good proportion of North 1 men at least appeared at the next Appell sporting armbands. The German Lager officer and his subordinates expressed curiosity, and when told it was in honor of the President of the United States who had died the day before they were even more curious. They had heard nothing from German sources, although later there was confirmation through the *Deutsche Rundfunk* and the one-page Barth newspaper. The question that must have been asked by many a Luftwaffe and Abwehr officer that evening was just how the prisoners knew before anyone else in camp. Having openly defied von Miller and his ferrets, we were not about to provide him with the answer, although his unease could be imagined. From past actions and questioning we had an idea he suspected an underground radio in the camp, and this act would double those suspicions. As previously mentioned, none of the radios were ever found by the Abwehr.

Even if hostilities did appear to be nearing an end, new prisoners and those transferred from other camps kept arriving at Barth. The total was now on the way to 9,000 and made the overcrowding in barracks more acute. The dormancy produced by starvation and cold was fast disappearing, and if order and discipline were to be maintained in the future we had to try to find something to keep the majority busy. New educational courses were set up in as many subjects as we could find tutors and pupil interest for. Sports and athletics were pursued with vigor, thanks mainly to the sports gear and hobby equipment that the International YMCA had been allowed to send in over past months. Athletics also served another purpose, to cover the training of men for our commando unit. Major T. A. G. Pritchard, a former British commando officer who had been captured in Italy, was actively teaching his trade to certain recruits, the US section being under a former infantry officer, Lieutenant Colonel Burt McKenzie. Our fate at the hands of the Germans still gave concern and we were determined to be prepared for the worst.

Everybody was encouraged to participate in some activity that didn't offend against the German camp regulations. To stimulate interest and set an example I decided the Senior Allied Officer should also participate. As the only sport of which I had much experience was boxing, I issued a challenge to anyone in the camp to go three two-minute rounds with me. No stipulations were made on weight, size, or experience. While it was always my policy to try to think carefully before taking decisions there were many lapses, and this was one of them. My boxing had been done in university days and apart from a fight in London early in 1943 it was ten years since regular ring appearances; and I was now 31 years old and not a nimble youngster. Even if our POW diet was hardly suited to building the strength of a prize fighter, there were big, robust fellows with boxing experience around who were not much more than half my age. Looking back it was a damn fool thing to do; I was asking for a beating. Not surprisingly, there was no shortage of prospective pugilists eager for a chance to knock the block off the Senior Allied Officer. For certain there were some who cherished the opportunity to swing a punch at Zemke with more than malice aforethought. Within a day of the announcement we had at least 50 names!

There was no going back; not that I had any intention but to go through with it. To ensure the selection was seen to be fair, all names of would-be opponents were written on slips of paper and Group Captain Weir asked to draw one from the hat. The chosen name was that of Major Cyrus Manierre, Gabreski's adjutant in North 3, a big lean US paratrooper who professed to have done a bit of boxing at West Point as a cadet. As can be seen from the particulars that were displayed in a Provisional Wing X bulletin, about the only advantage I had was experience.

Vital statistics of the two opponents:

	Colonel Zemke	vs	Major Manierre
Weight:	10 st. 10 lbs		11 st. 6 lbs
Height:	5 ft. 9 ins.		6 ft. 1 in.
Age:	31 years		25 years
Eyes:	Steel gray		Now dark blue
Hair:	Brown (graying)		Curly black
Training Diet:	Distilled water and cigar butts		Kriegbrot, Schnapps, schrimpers and rice
Ability:	55 bloody matches all in rings		Intercollegiate matches, street and bar-room clashes

A boxing card of ten matches constituted the afternoon program on 18 April with Manierre and myself winding up the main event. All contests brought rip-roaring action, and the show proved highly popular with the inmates of North 1 and those with special permission to attend. Ginger Weir, Einar Malstrom, and Cy Wilson acted as judges, "Tag" Pritchard as referee, and Gabby as backer (bookmaker). The betting was with IOUs. German staff attended and enjoyed seeing POWs pummel each other around the ring. The moment arrived when my opponent and I ducked under the ropes. My only misgiving was that I had not had any time to get in a little training to limber up. In the opening round the stringy Manierre showed a good straight left but began to tire and waste away after a few punches had been landed on his torso. In the second round he was decked with a solid right hook cross and from then on I carried him through the last round. Zemke received a unanimous decision for what was to be his last boxing match in any ring. Having Manierre as an opponent turned out to be a lucky draw, for from what I saw of the other boxers several could have dealt me out in the first round.

A few days after the boxing tournament I received a message to report to the Kommandant's office. On my arrival von Warnstedt motioned for me to sit down and said that he wanted to read me a teletype order that had arrived direct from the OKW. What I heard set my hair on end. The gist of the message was that all German personnel and prisoners of war were to be ready to evacuate Stalag Luft I within 24 hours notice, moving west to an undesignated location in the Hamburg area. Having witnessed the condition of the several groups of POWs who had walked to our camp from those further east, I viewed with dismay the prospects for our company of near 9,000. Owing to the devastated state of communications in the Reich such a move would almost certainly entail marching most, if not all, of the 150 miles. Added to this loomed the risk of being mistaken for an enemy column and attacked from the air. My lack of enthusiasm was made plain to the Kommandant as we discussed the ramifications of the proposed move.

Walking back to North 1 my thoughts led to the personal conviction that the POWs should sit tight. Stalag Luft I was not home in any sense but here we had sufficient food resources to keep the 9,000 fed for several weeks plus the other necessities of a spartan existence. To move at the eleventh hour, when the fast reducing area of the Reich under Nazi control was nearing chaos, would put many lives at risk.

Back in room 21 a staff meeting of Provisional Wing X was called with British seniors participating. The open discussion that resulted did not last long, for it was quickly apparent that those present were equally aghast at the proposed movement in the current uncertain war situation. For the first and only time in my military service a secret ballot was conducted amongst those present; the question, whether to submit or refuse if ordered to move out. The result was a firm stay put. Such blatant rejection could lead to solitary confinement for all present. Then there was the prospect of the Germans meeting our refusal to budge with force. McCollom's people had already picked up reports of an SS regiment assembling to the west near Rostock that might be brought here if there was trouble. Our commando people were alerted and a radio message of our intentions transmitted to London. The seniors went back to their compounds to spread the word that if ordered to move out we were staying put.

After considering whether or not to wait for the next move by the Germans on this development, I decided to take the initiative and go back to von Warnstedt immediately. Facing the Kommandant and deputy Jäger, there was no evasion or false diplomacy. They were told that the Allied senior officers and all prisoners in the camp objected to the proposed movement and insisted on remaining at Stalag Luft I until the cessation of hostilities. In the case of a "forced evacuation" any loss of life among POWs would inevitably be reported to the Allied powers with severe consequences for the perpetrators. Furthermore, neither I nor my staff would have a part in supervising such an evacuation. To my relief this defiance did not result in Zemke being whisked off to the cooler, as it undoubtedly would have done but a few weeks before. Instead reaction was generally mute, leaving me with the impression that the Luftwaffe staff did not want the task of moving 9,000 men across war-ravaged Germany either. How arrogant natures had mellowed!

Next day we learned from Pinky McCollom's informant in the German headquarters that the Kommandant had again spoken to his OKW contact. From what was heard it appeared that he reported the POWs' objection to moving and stated that his personnel were too few and lacked the transport and facilities to be able to conduct the large number of POWs held at Barth. Unless other orders were forthcoming he would continue to hold the prisoners here. No immediate response was forthcoming from the OKW. For the moment it looked as if we had won out on this matter, but rumors of von Warnstedt attending a conference with Reichsführer-SS Himmler present were worrying even if false.

In case the worst happened and we were faced with forced evacuation, no time was lost in preparing for such a contingency. Still the only senior officer with a pass, my hopping from compound to compound to confer with others seemed to go on continually during permitted hours. On one of these journeys Hauptmann Rath, the same Abwehr officer involved in the barracks search incident a few weeks before, approached me and asked to talk in private. Suspecting this was in regard to something connected with his ferrets' activities, I agreed and together we ambled round by the warning wire of the compound. To my complete surprise he offered me escape and escort to the US front lines with the only stipulation that he be turned over by me to the US authorities. He would provide a Luftwaffe uniform and the necessary papers. Finally, Rath pulled his revolver from its holster and handed it to me saying, "This is my pledge that I will uphold my part of the agreement." A few months ago such a proposal would have been jumped at. With such an escort it would have been easy to accomplish a getaway. Now, with the responsibilities of Senior Allied Officer, escape was out of the question. Smiling at Rath I handed him back his revolver saying, "Captain, you're a little late with your offer—you'd better keep this. You may have to use it." As Rath walked away I realized just how fearful many Germans were of the Soviets, now less than 100 miles from Barth.

That evening back in room 21 I had to engage in a little leg pulling by announcing to Hubbard, McCollom, and Greening that Zemke was leaving camp the next night with Hauptmann Rath headed west. Until they caught on their response was not nice.

The Abwehr ferret raids had now virtually ceased and with each passing day it became more evident that, in the absence of orders from higher command, von Warnstedt pursued his own course of action. We noted his men appeared to be requisitioning everything they could in the surrounding district for use in Stalag Luft I. For the inmates a continual air of suspense had developed, heightened by rumor. BBC broadcasts told POWs to remain where they were for liberation was near at hand, but we could see or hear little that told of its coming our way. True, the once little-used Barth airfield to the south now had a shuttle of Me 109 and FW 190 fighter bombers coming from and going to the east. We expected to see Soviet aircraft in the sky. Where were they? Strangely, none appeared.

Again taking the initiative, I directed McCollom to prepare three two-man teams equipped as best we could for escape. Once clear of the camp, each team had a separate objective: the British, American, and Russian front lines, with instructions to report to the highest authority they could contact on the status and situation at Stalag Luft I. For the teams going west their mission would be complete once they had fulfilled their instructions. The team going east was to attempt to bring back a Soviet liaison officer. Next, meeting with McKenzie and Pritchard, we established fixed objectives for the commando cadres when the time came for us to take over the camp. The first aim was to seize as many weapons as possible from German guards and storm the guard towers and arsenals. A barricade line would then be established across the neck of the peninsula to prevent any penetration of the camp. Special foraging crews were also organized ready to secure various requirements for the maintenance of camp life. Hopeful that our ear in the Kommandant's office would give warning of any impending orders to force our evacuation, we could only wait to see if it would be necessary to take the camp by force.

The three escape teams sent to the Allied lines went out on the night of 29 April. This was not a case of cutting barbed wire, for we were now able to grease palms and gates were opened to let "civilian workers" pass through. Neither was travel through the German countryside so hazardous in that few, if any, checks were now conducted; the once orderly society of the Nazi jackboot had been replaced by one of every man for himself. Refugees swarmed to the west. All three teams were successful in reaching their objectives. Neither were the Germans very concerned when six people were found missing at morning Appell next day. The camp authority was disintegrating fast.

Late that morning a telephone call to the gate of North 1 had the guard notify me that I was to report to von Warnstedt's office immediately. Was this the feared order to move camp or else? As I walked to the administrative area this ominous thought occupied my attention. Von Warnstedt was waiting on the steps of his office building, a rare occurrence indeed! As I approached he indicated that he wished me to accompany him on a walk outside the camp area. There was now no doubt that he had some crucial message to impart. Once well away from the main gate he broke his silence by saying: "Der Krieg ist jetzt über für uns" (the war is over for us). Then calmly he referred to my proposal when with the Swiss visitor we had previously walked together outside the camp. Would Provisional Wing X take over Stalag Luft I and permit all German personnel to leave without bloodshed? The intention was to go west as, like so many Germans, they preferred to be taken prisoner by the western Allies rather than the Soviets.

I could not have wished to hear sweeter words; my reply was a firm "yes," provided all his troops left together, took only small arms for personal protection, and did not attempt to destroy any of the camp facilities. To this he agreed and a mutually acceptable time for this departure was fixed—the coming midnight. All German personnel would be assembled outside the main camp gate by this hour. Also agreed was the necessity for his guards not to inform the POWs in advance. We shook hands on the deal. In contrast to his dejection, as we walked back my head spun with anticipation at the reception my news would bring. This was a development we had speculated on but not expected to be sprung so quickly. Little more was said before we parted and I returned to North 1.

With Greening, Hubbard, McCollom, and McKenzie gathered in room 21, POW guards were posted outside and told that no one was to enter or leave without my express permission. Shutting the door, all present were sworn to secrecy on what I was about to impart. Even if the guards outside did not hear my announcement that we would be free at midnight, they must have had a good idea that some favorable development was afoot when a chorus of jubilation broke out behind the closed door. On such occasions even those weighed down with the rank and responsibilities of colonels can be forgiven for behaving like a pack of juvenile football supporters gone wild at their team's victory. Once the hilarity had died down some serious discussion took place. First and foremost I did not want the camp POW population alerted to our forthcoming freedom, as this might create pandemonium. Inevitably some unruly elements would run amok and jeopardize the whole effort to have a bloodless takeover by seeking last-minute revenge on some unpopular German guard.

To keep control and order, knowledge of what was to happen must be kept to a few principals so that the majority of the camp would not make discovery until awakening next day. In case we had to enforce order McKenzie's and Pritchard's commandos must become military police. These men would have to be assembled in their respective compounds after darkness and given final instructions. One section would seize the Luftwaffe weapons armory from any time after 2300 hours and distribute weapons obtained to those other individuals who were to become guards and military police. At midnight, if not before, the guard towers would be taken over. Part of our defense force would move out to secure the peninsula neck as soon as von Warnstedt's column had passed. I wanted no Germans or displaced persons trying to seek sanctuary in the camp. Also, there was still the possibility that in a last vengeful act some Nazi officer might send his troops to exterminate some of us.

Leaving my friends to their preparations and walking through the administrative area to have a confidential meeting with the seniors in West compound, I noticed several indications of the Germans preparing to move. With Group Captain Weir and a group of seniors in West compound, a walk was taken round the compound boundary by the warning wire in a casual fashion so as not to alert other prisoners. Before disclosing that freedom was near I had to ask all to repress their emotions lest nearby POWs be attracted.

From the British it was learned that the adjacent flak school people had been observed destroying equipment, packing, and moving out. Now hardly a soul was to be seen on the site. Tag Pritchard was given the task of sending some of his commandos into the flak school that evening in the hope of finding weapons. Before departing, I assured Ginger Weir that someone would unlock the gates of West compound by 2300 hours so that he could join me to see our wardens depart. Next in North 2 and North 3 Cy Wilson and Gabby Gabreski were told of developments. Their people would play no part in the takeover but the seniors needed to be informed and put on their guard in case something went wrong.

Von Miller, who had been noticeably absent from the camp for a few weeks, suddenly reappeared. I was told he wanted to speak to me and, guessing he had word of what was to happen and might want to propose some offer that would gain him safe conduct or some other advantage, I returned word that I refused to see him. He had already approached Weir, who also would have nothing to do with him. Von Miller must have been in a desperate mood for—I later learned—he even had the audacity to see Marwood-Elton in the cooler, the former British Senior Officer of the camp whom he had helped put there! Of course he again received a rebuff.

Evening Appell and dinner moved with routine regularity for the majority, while for just a handful of kriegies the tension was acute. Von Warnstedt might keep his word, but would others? What of the Abwehr and the rebuked von Miller? As always in situations of concern, the minutes dragged by like hours. At dark the Luftwaffe guards moved in for the routine locking of barracks doors and closing window shutters with the exception of block number 9, but this evening for the first time the dog handlers and their canine companions were not to be seen in the inner compounds. The next two hours of waiting were almost unbearable, a state of mind that only those who have been confined for months, even years, can understand. At eleven o'clock on the dot the door of block 9 was opened and we moved out. McKenzie's men were soon to be seen scurrying around the camp in the darkness, for another good sign was that no searchlight illuminations were switched on. North 1 gates were found unlocked and Greening, Hubbard, McCollom, and Zemke passed through toward the main gate.

Our eyes having become accustomed to the dark, we could make out a large assembly outside on the road. In the flashlights that a few Germans were using an occasional glimpse of Luftwaffe uniforms and backpacks were to be seen. A few men appeared to be in civilian clothes. Some had bicycles laden with personal belongings and the few motor vehicles assigned to the camp were heavily overloaded with belongings. Presently we were joined by Ginger Weir, the other British seniors, and the commanders of North 2 and North 3. One didn't have to see faces to know their moods. The sheer glee of uplifted hearts came with every word uttered. Around ten minutes before the appointed hour for departure the Kommandant approached me. In the elation of the moment his exact words did not lodge in my memory, but they were to the effect that his party was about to move off. With a formal "Auf Wiedersehen" and a reciprocal military salute between us, he turned on his heels to walk back to his little sedan. I almost felt sorry for him as he and his motley bunch moved off.

We inheritors of Stalag Luft I stood talking and drawing on relaxing cigarettes, finding our moment of new-found freedom something of an anticlimax. Listening to the fading sounds of von Warnstedt's column as it wound its way to Barth, I could not help reflecting on my task at Stalag Luft I, in terms of personnel the largest "command" of my career. Unlike previous commands there had been no cases of AWOL, venereal disease, desertion, drunkenness, or any need to charge men for offenses against the local population; ironically, a saintly organization—thanks to the vigilance of the Germans.

7

Russky Come!

Freedom is a joyous thing and none more so than for those who have been closely confined for long periods. The first few minutes of May 1945 were spent savoring the exhilaration of the experience, just meddling around at the camp main gate. Gradually command responsibilities reasserted themselves in my thoughts. Our former keepers may have departed but war was still being waged. The facts were that we, 9,000 Anglo-Americans, held a small peninsula in enemy territory, and while it seemed highly unlikely that the Wehrmacht would appear to win it back, we were not yet completely liberated. More worrying was the information our people had been able to gather from the Germans that an SS detachment was waiting in the Zingst area to the north. Rumor had it that Himmler had been seen there a few hours past. The fear was that this SS outfit might have orders to attack our camp and then try to put the blame on the Soviets. There was even talk of them having Russian uniforms. We could only hope it was all just unfounded rumor.

Now in possession of the keys to most locks in Stalag Luft I, a first task was to release those prisoners in the cooler, in particular Group Captain Marwood-Elton and Colonel Russ Spicer who had been incarcerated in solitary confinement for many months. McCollom requested that he be allowed to release his close pal Spicer. My answer was short and simple, "Go man, go." Mac unlocked the iron door of the cell in the Stubenar-rest building and tiptoed up to the straw sack bunk. Tapping the sleeping Spicer on the shoulder he announced, "Hey Russ, it's time to get up. Let's go for a little walk." The still sleep-befuddled Spicer turned over grumbling, "This is a hell of a time to wake a living mortal." Finally coming to and recognizing McCollom in the candle light, his startled words of exclamation were, "What did they get you for, Mac?"

Six months of isolation and deprivation hadn't softened the resolve of this determined man. Neither had even harsher treatment and longer confinement broken the spirit of Marwood-Elton, once the Senior British Officer in our camp. Group Captain C. L. Greene turned the key that set this RAF officer free.

After catching some sleep, dawn found the occupants of room 21 commencing to move the headquarters of Provisional Wing X out of North 1 and into the former Luftwaffe administration buildings. These facilities, in comparison with our former restrictive quarters, were a luxury to say the least. We found proper mattresses and sprung beds to lie on, sheer joy after wood chips and reeds. There was sufficient room for all the sections of our organization both to work and live. Many of the Luft-waffe documents left behind made interesting reading. We also disco-vered IOUs for a total of nearly sixty thousand dollars of US and UK money which von Warnstedt and others had "borrowed" from the POWs!

With the blowing of numerous whistles by the compound command-ers, the POW day began as usual. To their surprise, when the kriegies assembled for roll call there were no Luftwaffe Lager people about. Instead they were greeted with catcalls and salutations from the guard towers where only yesterday sullen faces and machine guns were to be seen. The Germans were gone! Word spread like fire through tinder, fanned by exhilaration. COs requested that all men remain within the main boundary fences for the time being as the situation outside could be dangerous. The internal fences between the various compounds could come down. In short order these were demolished to diminish the feeling of confinement and allow a greater degree of socialization. However, my staff and I were well aware we were going to have great difficulty in keeping people in the camp and behind our barricaded peninsula. For many, the restraints and restrictions of months or years of this sandy flea-bitten place could not be shed quickly enough on that first day of freedom. Although Burt McKenzie had positioned his troops across the mile-wide neck of the peninsula, it was not difficult for any determined individual to slip across the fields unnoticed. The matter was further complicated in that, with the Soviets reported only a few miles away, the whole of the Barth area was reduced to near chaos.

Fear of the Russians and the general uncertainty as to what would happen when they arrived led the populace of the surrounding area to view the former American-British airmen's prison camp as a haven of civilized order. As anticipated, we were now beseeched with pleas for shelter from several groups of German civilians, foreign forced laborers, and deserting military types. Hard-hearted as it may seem, we could make no distinctions for there was no way of checking as to who we might be taking in. I only wanted ex-POWs in our enclave, for apart from there being more than enough problems with their welfare, holding outsiders of dubious nature might lead us into problems with the Soviets when they arrived. What with turning away people seeking to enter the camp, our guards were distracted from checking on ex-POWs leaving. In fact, with the guards having been prisoners themselves, a rather lax attitude existed, with the result that several hundred former kriegies disappeared into the local countryside during the first 48 hours of our takeover of the camp. Although anticipating the problem, I had not expected it to develop to the degree it did or realize what was happening, chiefly due to my preoccupation with other matters.

While we always had the closest liaison with the British, Provisional Wing X had been organized for the US personnel in Stalag Luft I. Now that the physical compound divisions were coming down and until all personnel were returned home, to ensure a more unified command Provisional Wing X should become Anglo-American. This was agreed with the British and Group Captain Weir was invited to be the chief of staff. The ever-diligent Mark Hubbard became assistant chief of staff instead of acting chief of staff, but as before he continued to shoulder the lion's share of the administrative work. Where the swastika flag had once hung, the Stars and Stripes and Union Jack proudly fluttered in the breeze outside the new Head Shed. Made by prisoners sewing together pieces of colored cloth, the Allied flags had been hidden away for just such an occasion.

An immediate concern was how to make contact with the advancing Russians, whose forward patrols were rumored to be close to Barth. We did not want our camp mistaken for an enemy stronghold, so the earlier we made ourselves known to the Soviet forces the better. So far there had been no news of the "escaped" scouts; we had no way of knowing if they had been successful in their mission. As soon as a vehicle we had found could be readied—with a Stars and Stripes on one fender and a white flag on the other—a German-speaking British officer and a Russian-speaking American officer were sent out with a tame civilian driver to scout the roads beyond Barth.

Another possibility of making contact with the Soviet forces was being explored by Wing Commander Blackburn, who had a team under his command manning the telephone exchange in the camp. By ringing numbers in Stralsund they hoped a phone would be answered by a Russian to whom news of our presence could be broken. A girl was still manning the Barth telephone exchange and she was asked to try the burgomaster of Stralsund. Her fearful reply was that the burgomaster had fled. How about a connection to the town hall of Barth was the next suggestion from our people, only to be told that the burgomaster and family had committed suicide by taking poison.

Also early in the day we had sent out teams with POW armed guards

to forage for flour, potatoes, and vegetables in the surrounding countryside. Transports were farm tractors and four-wheel carts left behind by
the Germans. Having no money to purchase, everything acquired was
appropriated under the threat of force. Another team led by Major Fred
Rabo had gone to Barth airfield to scout for gasoline or other material we
could use. All day there was much coming and going and exploration for
requisites and produce.

By early afternoon I felt it time to knock off for an hour or so from the
hubbub of the administration building and take a recreational walk outside the general camp area; in truth I too wanted to escape the encom-
passing wire fences and poke around. Ross Greening and a Captain J. D.
Harris, who had lived in our barracks, were invited to join me in taking
a look at the flak school to see how the Luftwaffe had lived. Reaching the
entrance gates, about a half mile from our camp, we marveled at the
quality of construction of the facility. Obviously a permanent installa-
tion, the brick and tile buildings were spacious, well lit and steam-
heated. The superb officers' mess with polished wood-block floor and
beautiful furniture showed that this was a military establishment of some
standing. There was evidence, however, that already some looting had
taken place. We entered a large airy gymnasium, again packed with all
the facilities one could wish. Here Greening found a javelin among the
strewn equipment. This caused him some delight as he had excelled with
the javelin when at college back in Washington State. This javelin, he
announced, would be his souvenir of two years at Barth.

We continued our wanderings, through another large mess hall and
into a well-equipped kitchen. The walls and floor were clad with white
ceramic tiles and the large steam ovens were of stainless steel. High-
quality kitchen utensils were stacked in profusion. I doubted if the Ritz
Hotel was so well equipped. Pondering how we POWs had cooked with
mostly homemade pots, I sauntered across the kitchen toward a counter-
like table. "Achtung!" In front of my eyes the barrel of a revolver
wavered; behind it a deranged countenance. With that first shock the
mind did not question if it was fear or anger facing me. A glimpse of
Luftwaffe uniform triggered my response, "What the hell are you doing

here still?" It was automatically assumed that the young officer who had been hiding behind the counter, and who now threatened to extinguish my existence, was a leftover from the flak school establishment. To my great relief the answer wasn't a bullet. In a quavering voice he launched into a long explanation that he was simply looking for food, having been traveling on foot from the east for several days. Buoyed up by this show of timidity, I told him we were part of a company of former prisoners of war who were searching the building. Any shots would bring armed men running and he could expect no mercy. Of course this was bluff; I had no idea where our nearest guards were; the only weapon between the three of us was Ross Greening's recently acquired javelin. Thankfully neither of my companions tried any heroics to save the situation, and with a quick word in English I asked them not to try. Continuing with the firm line that appeared to placate the German, I told him I was an American colonel and was not interested in capturing him. If he gave me his gun he could go on his way. No one was more surprised than Mrs. Zemke's little "Hoo-bert" when the young officer meekly lowered his gun and handed it over. Perhaps the fact that I had spoken to him in German from the outset had calmed his fears.

Who knows, had I used English that nervous finger might have tightened on the trigger. I'd been in this place once before—looking down the barrel of a revolver—and didn't relish it one little bit. The Luftwaffe lieutenant then pleaded that the weapon was only drawn in self-defense and that without it he feared for his life as he fled from the Russian hordes. We escorted this pathetic fellow out of the building. As we walked I removed the bullets from his gun and returned it to him saying the Soviets were already in our camp—more bluff—and that he had best leave the flak school as fast as his legs could carry him. For some impulsive reason of sympathy for his plight, as he bade us farewell I said "Here" and gave him the handful of bullets just removed. I don't know who was the most surprised, the Luftwaffe officer or my two companions. The former had a look of amazement on his face as he thanked me and made off across the fields. My friends said nothing but I bet they were thinking "How dumb can a colonel get?"

Following the departure of the fleeing Luftwaffe officer it suddenly occurred to me that we *did* have armed guards close by at the Red Cross parcel store. Because the German prison regulations would not allow Red Cross parcels to be stored in the camp, arrangements had been made for all these supplies to be kept in a large warehouse at the flak school. One of our officers kept an inventory of all parcels received and removed, chiefly to watch for pilfering by the Germans. During April there were several occasions when Luftwaffe staff or someone who could obtain access to the store had rifled a number of parcels. As usual, our protests did little to improve security. At last we could guard the place ourselves. Or so I thought, for having decided to take a look at the store we rounded a corner to see the warehouse besieged by some 50 German civilians, some trying to force the doors. No sign of any guards. Pushing through the crowd to the battered doors, we asked a short, stocky German who appeared to be the ringleader what he thought he was doing. Shouting something about there being food in the building which they were going to get, he continued to force the door. Told that this was a store of Red Cross food exclusively for the POWs in the adjacent camp, "To hell with those heathens," he screeched, "The food is now ours!"

Having once only narrowly escaped a lynching at the hands of German civilians I was careful not to antagonize this motley bunch. Most were middle-aged and none appeared to have firearms, but three of us with a javelin were hardly likely to endure if the mob turned hostile. We moved discreetly to one side, and Captain Harris was instructed to run as hard as he could to our camp and collect a group of armed MPs. He was further instructed to have them fire in the air as they approached in the hope of scaring the looters. While Harris sped away, Greening and I stood watching as the doors were finally breached and the men entered the building. There they began to break open the plywood packing cases in which the parcels were shipped, each individual emerging with a parcel under each arm, about all that could be carried by one person.

From my observations it was fairly clear that the stocky ringleader knew exactly what was what. He wore civilian clothes but I had a pretty good idea he had been one of the Luftwaffe or Abwehr men at Stalag

Luft I. When von Warnstedt's column had moved out the previous night we had a party of our commandos follow them at a discreet distance to a point west of Barth town to ensure they really were on their way. No doubt some individuals with local connections had slipped away from the column in the darkness to remain in the vicinity. This individual must have been one such and had informed some of his acquaintances in Barth that he knew a source of real coffee, chocolate, and cigarettes.

A volley of rifle fire announced the approach of a dozen POW MPs. The shooting had the desired effect, for the looters took off in great haste. Most thought we would shoot to kill and, life being of more concern than food, in their efforts to escape parcels were discarded as they fled across the fields. My orders, however, were simply to shoot above them. The only object was to instill the fear of God so they didn't return.

The Senior Allied Officer was not in a good mood when he returned to camp. Luther Richmond, whose task it had been to administer the Red Cross parcels, and Burt McKenzie were carpeted and a few tail feathers extracted for their negligence in failing to safeguard our vital store. Richmond was told to round up as many men as he needed and move the 50,000 parcels from the flak school building and into our camp where they would be stored safe and sound. My wrath having subsided, a discussion with McKenzie ensued about tightening up his guards. Understandably, one could not expect former POWs with a minimum of training to become transformed into super-efficient military police. Given their limitations, there was still no excuse for the casual attitude to their duties evident this day. McKenzie and Richmond, both good people, probably went away muttering under their breath about the ungrateful SOB who wielded the big stick. Sure it was tough on our first day of liberty to have your ears burned. But we just had to tighten the whole setup or we were headed for big trouble.

Scores of civilians were still arriving at the main gate pleading for sanctuary because "Russky come!" There was even a deputation from Barth asking us to occupy the town. Such was their fear of the Russians. We learned that advanced patrols had been seen approaching from Stralsund, but our scouts had so far not returned having made contact. Late in the day two South Africans, Major Braithwaite and Flight Sergeant Korson, were sent out when another report said Soviet troops were five miles south of Barth. All these people were volunteers, for another rumor held that the Russians shot at anything or anybody seen on the roads.

To add to our problems, in the late afternoon the electrical power to the camp suddenly ceased. Without electricity the well pumps providing our water were useless and the sewage disposal system no longer functioned. Inconvenient, if of lesser concern, was the prospect of no lighting that coming night. Two armed parties were sent out, one to Barth to try and discover why the power had failed and the other into the flak school to look for any auxiliary electrical generators. The Barth party returned to say that electricity was not generated locally and that the power lines had been cut by the retreating Wehrmacht to hinder the Russians. Tag Pritchard's men had better luck and found a diesel generator in the flak school. By next morning we had lines rigged to provide sufficient power to run our pumps and provide fresh water again, although insufficient power for lighting.

For the time being candles were brought out again and flickered in the new Wing Headquarters of Wing X—with the Germans gone we had dropped the Provisional tag. Before midnight the guards at the main gate arrived to announce excitedly that Braithwaite and Korson had returned in a truck with two Russians. Hearing cheers we went to meet them and greet Lieutenant Alec Karmyzoff, an infantryman who, we learned, had started out at Stalingrad in 1942 and been fighting his way west ever since. Our two scouts told excitedly of their meeting with these first Soviet patrols. Passing several groups of refugees on the road south of Barth, they came to a crossroads and face to face with a chunky little Russian brandishing a regular arsenal of weapons. "Engliski, Engliski," our scouts shouted and were taken to Lieutenant Karmyzoff. Despite language difficulties the Russian officer got the message and decided to come and see for himself. We made his welcome as best we could and offered him a bed. He refused point blank to sleep on any German bed and made himself comfortable on the floor! We could give him some good news when he awoke—the BBC broadcast that night that Hitler was dead.

With a Russian officer at hand, the seniors of the camp decided to set out early next morning to try and make contact with the main Russian force as they approached Barth. In addition to the Russian, Weir, Greening, Pritchard, myself, and Delarge, our interpreter, were to travel in the German Jeep-like vehicle we had acquired. At 0500 hours, just as we were about to leave, one of our scouts, Captain P. Robertse, and a Pole acting as interpreter, who had "escaped" during the night before we took over the camp, returned with another Russian officer, Major Svintsov. Contact had been made at Stralsund, 20 miles to the east of Barth. Svintsov entered the camp to a rousing greeting from the ex-kriegies, word soon having spread that the Russkys had arrived. After exchanging salutations, we were told by the major that there would be no problems providing our men kept out of the way and did not hinder the Soviet advance. Although there were no pockets of German resistance in the area, it was expected some last-ditch encounters with the SS further west might occur. Learning that the main Soviet drive had bypassed Barth to the south, but that a contingent was on its way to occupy the town, we decided to carry on with our proposed trip and Major Svintsov accompanied us.

Passing directly through the center of Barth on this beautiful clear May morning we were amazed and amused to see how quickly the townsfolk had changed allegiance. The white sheets hanging from windows we could understand, but in many places makeshift Soviet flags fluttered from poles. I drove and Svintsov held down the other front seat as we sped over cobbled roads toward Labnitz, a village on the way to Stralsund. We hoped the Stars and Stripes and white flags on the fenders would save us from becoming a target—there was a real possibility that at a distance we might be mistaken for a hostile vehicle. At last, far ahead on an open stretch of road, we saw figures approaching. Bringing our vehicle to a halt, Major Svintsov and the rest of the party got out and started on foot toward the oncoming troops. Then we decided it would be more prudent to stop and wait for our liberators to reach us. Slowly they approached in single file, walking in a rather casual manner; surprisingly so considering there might have been an enemy ambush ahead.

The Soviet major stood in the middle of the road while we sat on the edge of a culvert until the first soldiers reached us. A discussion developed between an officer in the leading element and our major and it transpired that we were to wait where we were while the advance continued toward Barth.

As we whiled away the time, basking in the warmth of the spring sunshine, the road began to fill with all kinds of military traffic streaming west. With the intermittent groups of tramping soldiers came small vehicles, personnel carriers, and large trucks. There were many horse-drawn wagons carrying all sorts of equipment, some with women who were obviously camp followers. More foot soldiers appeared plodding in the fields parallel to the road. Often the Russian soldiers would show curiosity at our little group, occasionally raising a hand as they passed. After perhaps an hour, we heard the tooting of horns and looking east saw a couple of Jeeps weaving their way through the troops. On reaching us they stopped and from behind the wheel of the lead Jeep a tall weather-beaten officer got out and approached. Svintsov introduced him to the Anglo-American presence as Colonel T. D. Zhovanik (pronounced Cher-vor-nick), a regimental commander of the 65th Soviet Army. I received a typical Russian greeting of a bear hug and a kiss on each cheek plus a broad smile and the salutation "Americanski, you are now free!" Having experienced the suspicion of foreigners which seems to be inherent in Russians, I deemed it prudent to take this opportunity to express in glowing terms our gratitude at being liberated.

Another help in establishing good rapport was my ability to stammer out a few words in Russian, remembered from my days in the Soviet Union. Following further introductions to members of Zhovanik's staff, we chatted about the German situation and offered a few cigarettes. Then Colonel Zhovanik proposed a celebration. Beckoning to Weir and myself to hop in his lend-lease Jeep, he sped off with us down the road toward Barth. With the other vehicles following, we weaved in and out of the marching troops until we came to a crossroads. Adjacent to this junction, surrounded by large trees, stood a modest brick farmhouse.

Without hesitation the colonel drove straight up the driveway, as if he had been there many times before. With a few curt orders to his men, the entire dwelling was cleared of the bewildered farming family by the simple expedient of brandishing weapons and uttering threats which needed no interpretation to be understood. These folk were driven from their home like hogs from a pen, an act alien to my western code of conduct with civilians. Yet having learned something of the devastation and suffering the war had brought to the USSR, I could understand this lack of compassion.

Seemingly from out of nowhere a large Russian soldier appeared and, while he talked with his colonel, produced a white apron which he tied about his hefty midsection; undoubtedly a chief cook. While we were ushered into the front room of the house, other soldiers investigated the cupboards and drawers to find a tablecloth, napkins, china, and cutlery to set the large wooden table. Most intriguing to us westerners was the ease with which the Soviet infantryman just propped his rifle against a wall and happily became a waiter. Soon trays filled with bottles were carried in. My heart dropped when a bottle of vodka and the proverbial one-shot glass caught my eye. The victors had obviously come prepared as this liquor would not have been found in a German farm cupboard. We were about to indulge in one of those wild drinking sessions at which the Russians are without doubt world masters. Having experienced these bashes, I made an attempt to warn my western cohorts of the dangers they now faced. To no avail; and why should Zemke try and put the dampers on their first opportunity for a real celebration in a long while. And so it went, Stalin, Churchill, Truman, Eisenhower, Rokosoffski, and just about everyone you could think of who had taken on the Nazis.

Soon we were invited to sit before the biggest spread most of us had seen for a long time. Fried chicken, potatoes, vegetables garnished an overladen table. Undoubtedly from the unfortunate farmer's own pantry. In truth I cannot remember much more about the function other than that it terminated with Zhovanik, Zemke and staff departing for Barth in an open carriage drawn by a pair of horses and driven at a fast clip by a Russian. Greening was slumped in a corner feeling very ill. The worst sufferer was poor Ginger Weir; twice we had to stop to allow the group captain to accommodate himself of the "dry heaves." When we reached Barth the buggy proceeded to the town hall where Zhovanik and other happy members of his staff departed. While our celebration had been in progress, a regimental forerunner had secured the building for use as a local headquarters. The townsfolk peeped out from behind window blinds. One can imagine them wondering just what kind of conquerors had descended upon them.

After being delivered to the main gate of the camp by our Soviet horseman, there were some of us who would dearly have liked to seek the solitude of their bunks for the rest of the day. There was, however, need to discuss matters raised with the Soviets, most importantly the repatriation of 9,000 POWs.

During these discussions a commotion was noticed coming from the area of the main gate, although there was nothing unusual in this with the guards having to prevent people from leaving or entering unless authorized. Suddenly the door of the conference room was swung open violently with a loud bang. Looking up I beheld a small Russian soldier in riding boots, crumpled uniform, and a cossack hat, but my gaze immediately shifted to the large revolver that he was wielding. He was shouting incoherently and showed considerable rage. Now one of the penalties of being the bossman is that in such situations everyone expects him to speak. Thus when I attempted to placate the interloper with the few welcoming words of Russian I knew, the revolver barrel was immediately pointed at me. To add to my discomfort there was a distinct click of the hammer as the weapon was cocked. The experience of dealing with a similar situation the previous day was no consolation: the realization that the outraged Cossack was the worse for drink made this confrontation far more precarious.

When I asked Lieutenant Durakov, our Russian-speaking US officer, what the man was saying, he mumbled something about the Russian wanting to know why the prisoners were not released from the camp. Seeing that the revolver was aimed at Zemke, several of my stalwart deputies took the opportunity to slide behind doors or dive out of windows. Further escapes were halted by the little major waving the revolver in a wide arc with unintelligible but obvious threats of intent. Unfortunately, the aim of the weapon returned to me. Steeling myself to keep calm and moderate my tone of voice, I made an attempt to tell the enraged drunk that this was no longer a prison camp. Whether the tubby Durakov couldn't understand him or was too petrified to translate, we were making little progress. Fortunately someone said that Flight Lieutenant Delarge, who spoke excellent Russian, had been sent for. In the meantime I just prayed that my attempts to talk to the major would at least stop him from shooting—which he looked certain to do at any moment. I gathered he thought we were Germans. This was denied by Delarge when he arrived.

The gist of the drunken little soldier's ranting was that we were still holding prisoners against their wills, otherwise the barbed wire fences would have been pulled down and the gates opened. He was going to see the prisoners were set free. It suddenly occurred to me that here was the way out; let him liberate the prisoners. Delarge was told to tell the Russian that he could have the honor of being their liberator and that I would accompany him into the North compound and tell the men so. Immediately a change of mood was evident; we even got a smile from this red-eyed face. Word was passed ahead by runner to North 1 compound to gather as many people as possible at the gate and to cheer the Russian when we arrived. At the first opportunity this little roughneck was to be given "the old blanket treatment."

Walking out with the gun-toting Cossack, I found he had a companion and a camp follower–type girlfriend, all on horseback. Mounting up, my would-be terminator indicated that I should walk ahead while he and his friends trotted along behind. At least a couple of hundred ex-kriegies had been gathered at the entrance to the North compound as the party approached. Overcome by the welcome, the Russian cased his pistol and dismounted. In a flash, he, his cohort, and his girlfriend were seized and disarmed. Spread blankets, held firmly at each corner, were produced and the startled Russians thrown into the center and tossed in the air. Each time they came to ground they were tossed up again to a resounding cheer from the crowd. After a dozen ups and downs the anticipated happened; both drink-soaked characters became violently ill. Thus pacified, the Russians and their now frightened girlfriend were all dragged off to the cooler to sober out in solitary confinement.

The amazing part of all this was that our main gate guards let these people in the camp and showed them to our headquarters. What was the point of sentries who were intimidated and cooperated so easily? Some harsh words were passed on to the commander of the MPs and, lest some other Russians arrived to liberate us, I had the remaining inner compound gates and fencing torn down. Colonel Zhovanik's office was telephoned and told that we had again been liberated. His men collected the three intruders. I never heard what happened to them and thought it best not to ask.

Next morning found new problems for the senior Allied officers. In our absence the previous day, a couple of tragedies had come to light. MP guards who had been patrolling around the estuary edge discovered the bodies of five German civilians lying in rushes. Three women and two young children, all shot through the temple. How could such a ghastly incident happen within our sphere of control? While it was conceivable that these people had somehow managed to slip by our guards and get onto the peninsula, it was inconceivable that any ex-POW, however much he hated the Germans, would murder helpless women and children. A special investigation committee was put on the case but they never resolved the mystery satisfactorily. Although no weapon could be found, mass suicide appeared the only answer.

Further disheartening news for me came in a report of three casualties among our ex-kriegie populace. Three men out on an unauthorized night's spree had commandeered a small car and gone joyriding. In the process they had found a supply of liquor. Ultimately they had crashed into a ditch at high speed and all three died of the multiple injuries sustained.

To try and give our people some recreation in the surrounding countryside we arranged for the issue of 90 daily passes, clearing this with the Soviet authorities in Barth. There were still men who said to hell with authority and made their own way out. It was easy enough to sling a few timbers together and make a raft to cross the estuary. Many had aspirations of finding cooperative female company, which I thought most unlikely in the frightened population around Barth. One should not underestimate the male with amorous intentions, for it was passed around that among the foreign workers at the former chemical works across the bay were some very friendly French women. Evidently there were successful liaisons—if successful is the right word—as before we left Barth our doctors were reporting cases of VD.

8

Lager in Limbo

At midday I had my first formal meeting with Colonel Zhovanik at his Barth headquarters. The session went well and it was clear he was going out of his way to be helpful. Before leaving I invited him to come and inspect our camp. To show him our facilities and status, it was decided to take his small party on a walking tour of the camp. First, to provide a little pomp for his benefit, a guard of honor made up of a British and American contingent, unarmed but provided with the cleanest tunics we could scrounge from the remaining Red Cross supplies. This created quite an impression with Zhovanik—as it did with other Soviet dignitaries who visited Stalag Luft I at later dates. As we intended, it gave the impression that this ex-POW establishment stood as a military unit and not as a shambles of misdirected war survivors.

A hasty tour of the compounds gave Zhovanik a fleeting review of the general living conditions of the average kriegie. The compound commanders being alerted of his visit were instructed to call their people to attention and salute when he entered their patch. I doubt if he'd received as many cheers, salutations, or military salutes in his three years of combat as on this particular day. Later, with a sparkle in his eye he asked: "Do all westerners cheer and salute as much as your troops do?" I only smiled at him, for I knew he was well aware that all these gestures were for his particular ego. After visiting the dispensary and the general base workshops taken over from the former camp authorities, we wound up in our officers' club. Sitting down to partake of crumpets, coffee, and jam from a Red Cross parcel, we turned to the requirements of our commands.

Here I found Zhovanik an emphatic man; he didn't digress, coming straight to the point. Quite unlike meetings with Soviet officers during my earlier stay in Russia. There they tended to vacillate and go to higher headquarters for decisions. Often when in doubt they would ask questions rather than answer them: a favorite trick. Zhovanik confirmed his appointment as commander of Soviet forces with the job of restoring order in the Barth area. He looked to us for cooperation and to keep our people out of the way of his troops. In turn I acknowledged his position as the occupying power and assured him that to the best of our ability we would keep our people in check. To better ensure harmony, the exchange of liaison officers to be on hand at each headquarters was proposed.

Having established a rapport with this likable and astute man, I felt a word of complaint could be edged into the conversation. Yesterday one or two of our foraging parties had been stopped by Russian soldiers who had confiscated tractor, trailer, and weapons. Protests were met with the leveling of submachine guns. Our people, recognizing the Russians were not in a mood to argue, wisely complied. This seemed to amuse the colonel, who advised that if we required anything send word and his troops would provide. Taking immediate advantage of his generosity, a request was made that we be allowed to forage for meat, flour, and potatoes. This Zhovanik accepted if we provided a hundred of our men to do the fetching and carrying. Before departing he raised the incident of the liberating Cossack. He seemed genuinely surprised that we hadn't

The grand boxing tournament of 18 April 1945. Among the spectators were the chief Luftwaffe administrators of the camp. Kommandant Oberst von Warnstedt is leaning forward; his number two, Oberstleutnant Jäger, is on his left. Directly behind von Warnstedt sits Lieutenant Colonel Hankey, RAMC, our highly esteemed medical officer.

Round 1. The contestants square up. Neither of us had any surplus weight but Manierre had extra height and reach.

My second, Captain Cal Reeder, another fighter pilot from the 56th Group, giving me instructions. Notice the damage to the bridge of my nose caused by a good straight jab from Manierre.

Round 2. Manierre on the ground while referee T. A. G. Pritchard makes the count and a relieved SAO takes a breather on the ropes. In the audience, directly behind me, sit the Luftwaffe staff and Ross Greening (legs crossed).

HEADQUARTERS
Provisional Groups II and III
Stalag Luft I, Barth, Germany

Sept. 18, 1944

Subject: Submission of Insigna Design
To   : Col. E.A.Malmstrom
        Group II
        Commanding

      1. The attached insignia was designed here in camp for the "X" Provisional Wing and is hereby submitted for approval.

      2. Explanation of the insignia follows, in detail:

      The ARMORED HELMET & SWORD in heraldic symbols stands for the fighting profession and is representative of the combat airmen and crews here in camp.

      The DIAGONAL dividing the insignia means a bastard or mixed group or family. This divides the wire barb and the propellars into sections.

      The COLORS were picked so the BLACK could represent the dark side, or prison side(wherein the barbed wire is mounted) and the long nights here due to being so far north. The WHITE showing a contrast for the free life with the propellars and could also represent the short days (so far north).

      The BARB from the wire represents prison life and also having the "X" shape with extended pointed prongs makes a symbolic "X" represent the "X" Provisional Wing.

      The PROPELLARS being five in number represent the five provisional groups in this wing, and the BLOOD RED COLOR standing for the wounds and those not so lucky; but all brought into combat and here by propellars.

      The GREEK on the scroll is characteristic to most coats of arms. This Greek "FINI FRATER" means "Finished, Brother" --- and, I believe, is self-explanatory.

      SILVER was chosen for the metal border, helmet, sword, diagonal, scroll, etc., as silver in the army is considered higher than gold. The sword hilt, however, is gold, as are the wings on the helmet and propellar hubs.

A.A. SMEDLEY, JR.
Capt., A.C.

                    1st Ind.
Hqtrs Prov. Group II, Prov. Wing "X", Barth, Germany. 9/18/44
To: Col. BYERLY, Prov. Wing "X", COMMANDING.

      1. For your information.

E.A. MALMSTROM
Col., A.C.
Group II
Commanding

The winning insignia of Provisional Wing X designed by Captain Art Smedley, together with the explanation of the design that he submitted.

A photo picked up in the Luftwaffe barracks after the Germans left. It shows a typical bunch of guards, mostly near-middle-aged men and generally not well educated.

One of our MPs in a guard tower shortly after the Germans left. No, he is not fat, his jacket is flapping open.

Our people were not long in opening up gaps in the outer guard fences.

The store building in the flak school shortly after it had been looted by German civilians. Two of our MPs walk by.

Two photos joined to give a panorama of the camp looking north. The building in the foreground is the bathhouse. The compound beyond is North 1, and barracks 9, my abode, is that on the left center of compound area, end door facing camera. White patches on windows are pieces of cardboard taken from Red Cross parcels to replace broken glass. On extreme right, foreground, are dirt heaps, all that remained after the mess hall fire. A sprinkling of snow and ice round the pond show that the Baltic winter had not departed even in late April.

Soccer match on the West compound parade ground shortly after our liberation. Any attempt to hang a coat on the boundary fences during our imprisonment would have quickly brought a bullet.

The kriegie jazz band was good and could play outside in the warmer May days. It helped to keep up morale during our frustrating wait for evacuation.

Official Russian inspection of Stalag Luft I, 4 May 1945. Left to right: Colonel Zhovanik, Zemke, General Borisov, and Group Captain Cecil Weir, chief of staff Provisional Wing X.

Visit of more Soviet commanders, 8 May 1945. Our interpreter, Flight Lieutenant Delarge, RAF, on left; General Marozil, Red Army; Zemke; Marozil's aide; and Einar Malstrom who, like me, wears a black mourning band for President Roosevelt.

Honor guard of British and American MPs for the departure of General Marozil in a lend-lease Jeep. Notice the general enjoys an American cigarette we gave him and that his bodyguard totes a tommy gun.

The Russian pass that gave me permission to do anything I wanted around Barth.

With the Soviet commanders in the former Luftwaffe headquarters at Stalag Luft I, 4 May 1945. Flight Lieutenant Delarge, our interpreter, shares a joke with a senior Russian officer. Next to him are Major General Borisov, myself, and Second Lieutenant J. S. Durakov, our other interpreter. Standing behind are Ginger Weir and Colonel Zhovanik.

This attractive Soviet woman with the fetching smile was present at several gatherings we had with General Borisov. I asked Zhovanik about her: "This is the general's property, so beware," he said with a smile. Thus warned, I saw to it that our people treated her with respect and did not try to get too familiar. What her medals were for is open to speculation!

A shot taken outside the Russian headquarters in Barth. Left to right: Colonel Zhovanik, Major T. A. G. Pritchard, Major General Borisov, Lieutenant Colonel Mark Hubbard (then Wing X liaison officer with the Soviets), and Flight Lieutenant Delarge, the Polish RAF interpreter.

Abandoned by the Luftwaffe on Barth airfield were several different aircraft types, including the He 111, FW 190, and Ju 88 seen here. Jets were assembled in the hangars by forced labor. From here 1st Air Division B-17s repatriated us to France and England.

Barth airfield was a permanent Luftwaffe base and had good buildings. The operations block even included an exterior clock. In this pose Mark Hubbard and Zemke stand with Soviet officers shortly before our evacuation from Barth. Zhovanik is on my left.

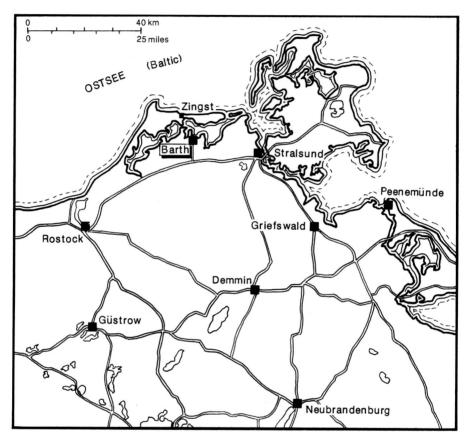

Location of Barth.

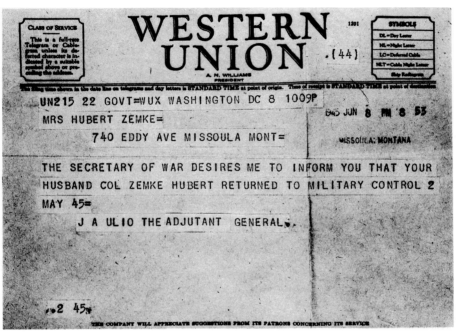

UN215 22 GOVT=WUX WASHINGTON DC 8 1009P

1945 JUN 8 PM 8 53

MRS HUBERT ZEMKE=

740 EDDY AVE MISSOULA MONT=

MISSOULA. MONTANA

THE SECRETARY OF WAR DESIRES ME TO INFORM YOU THAT YOUR
HUSBAND COL ZEMKE HUBERT RETURNED TO MILITARY CONTROL 2
MAY 45=

J A ULIO THE ADJUTANT GENERAL.

2 45

Better late than never! This official telegram didn't reach my folks in Montana until 8 June 1945, by which date I'd already talked with my wife on a couple of occasions by radio from Europe.

Unbeknown to me, Pete Dade and the boys of my old fighter group back at Boxted, England, were paying me the most flamboyant compliment I've ever received. It was an emotional moment when I set eyes on this P-47 under the Eiffel Tower.

A French Fieseler Storch, believed to have been one of the six that comprised "Zemke's Air Force."

OFFICER'S PAY DATA CARD

bert Zemke, Col AC-RA   O-22353

(Name)   (Serial number)   (Grade and arm or ser

r 9 years' service ____ 6th ____ pay period __9__ years

Feb, 19 45

nthly base pay and longevity _____ $ 416.(

l pay for Flying   208.

lowances _____   120.(

sistence 30 day month   42.(

Date 10 July 1945 Total, $ 787.(

pendents (state names and addresses):
Maria Zemke, 740 Eddy Avenue
Missoula, Montana

idence of dependency (mother) filed with voucher No. _

_____, 19 _____

counts of _____

lotments, class E, $ 18.05 $ 250.00 $

surance, class D, $ _____   Class N, $ 9.(

y reservations, class B, $ 75.00 _____

her deductions, $ _____

bsequent changes in above data with dates thereof:

_____

In mid-July 1945 they finally got my pay situation sorted out. The allotments were to my wife and a savings scheme. It shows why every officer was keen to keep up his flight status.

Now in Air Force blue, three aces of the 56th Fighter Group who all spent the final days of the war in Stalag Luft I meet up again at Albany Air Force Base, Georgia, in 1958. Gerald W. Johnson and Francis S. Gabreski are at left and Hub Zemke at right. With them is Colonel John R. Alison (second from right), an ace from the Chinese and Burmese campaign. Alison and Zemke had served together in the Soviet Union.

In 1963 while serving in Spain I had the opportunity to meet two of the great Luftwaffe aces: Colonel Walter Krupinski, credited with 197 victories (left) and Colonel Eric Hartman (right) with 352 victories. Both had amassed the greater part of their high totals on the Russian front.

shot the fellow. It was explained that neither I nor any of my staff carried weapons. Furthermore we wished to avoid any action that might mar relations with our liberators. I felt we had made a good impression with Zhovanik but the number of incidents already reported in the countryside involving our people and Soviet soldiers, although minor, underlined the importance of putting a liaison officer in the local Russian HQ as soon as possible. The man for the job was Lieutenant Colonel Mark Hubbard. Mark was off early next day with Flight Lieutenant Delarge to take up his duties. On arrival an early question to Zhovanik was where they should put their bedrolls. The Russian colonel said to look round the square and pick a place they liked. Hubbard made his choice, assuming he would be lodged with a family. He was aghast when Zhovanik had his troops evacuate the unfortunate occupiers onto the street. Hubbard immediately observed that it didn't pay to lose a war.

The military philosophy of requisitioning anything and everything they wanted typified the Soviet presence as occupiers of this defeated land. Surprisingly for a system where the individual could easily run up against the stern rulings of the state, a large proportion of the Red Army troops we initially encountered seemed to do as they wished. The common soldier roamed the countryside around Barth plundering whatever took his fancy in the first few days of occupation, as if it was deliberate policy to terrorize and subjugate. I came to the conclusion that many had long ago become separated from their units and had fought their way into Germany with the advancing front as itinerants. One could understand that after the pillage of mother Russia there would be little charity extended toward the German populace. Indeed, if civilians resisted they were shot.

At first the Soviet soldiers were just as likely to take something they wanted from ex-kriegies encountered as they were from German civilians. My complaints to Zhovanik resulted in his sending us German vehicles and other equipment to make up for that appropriated, but we continued to suffer some confiscations. Most difficulty was experienced by Major Fred Rabo and his team, who had been working hard at the airfield to make it serviceable again. This large permanent former Luftwaffe station offered the best exit for the 9,000 ex-kriegies, and in my first meeting with Zhovanik he had accepted the likelihood of our evacuation by air and given us responsibility for the airfield. Of course, in clearing obstructions and booby traps we were saving the Soviets the job. Rabo experienced a continuing problem with roaming Russian troops bent on locating fuel and equipment left by the Luftwaffe, even though the Barth command had said the airfield was to be immune from interference.

On Friday 4 May, Rabo's crew had a runway clear and a flying control team installed so that he could declare the field operational. The Luftwaffe had departed in a hurry, leaving 18 fused 250 kg HE bombs spaced out across the grass as a deterrent. The nimble fingers of Second Lieutenant H. C. DeLury successfully removed all fuses. With the aid of horses and a wood sled the bombs were dragged to the edge of the airfield. A booby trap bomb found in the gasoline storage looked too tricky for our amateur bomb disposal team to remove, but with ultra caution was eventually made safe. On the airfield there were 38 aircraft of a dozen different types that the Germans had abandoned. They included four Ju 88s in airworthy condition and several other planes that needed little work to restore. The only aircraft the Luftwaffe had attempted to destroy were a few Arado 234 jets that they appeared to be assembling in the hangars. Rabo's men painted red stars over the original nationality marks on all the aircraft, which greatly pleased the Russians.

A grim discovery was made at the airfield on the first day. Standing between a Luftwaffe mess and workshops were three two-story barracks buildings surrounded by barbed and electrified fencing. This proved to be a concentration camp for mainly Greek and French civilian prisoners who had offended against the Nazi regime and had been employed in some kind of forced labor factory adjacent to the airfield. About 2,000 emaciated prisoners were found in these buildings, many dead or dying. The bodies of those who had recently expired lay rotting on their bunks. The living were too weak to move them. Doc Hankey and his medics, who first inspected the site, said that such human degradation as they found was almost unimaginable. The stench of decomposing bodies and human excreta was sickening. Many of these poor creatures were so helpless they had lain in their own mess for days. Disease was rife. Hankey immediately put the place out of bounds, fearing an epidemic. He utilized the airfield hospital in an attempt to save some lives, recruiting a few German girls as nurses.

According to our medics the daily ration for each concentration camp inmate was totally inadequate. They came to the conclusion that these people were being deliberately and slowly starved to death. At the time we had not heard about such infamous places as Belsen, and the existence of the Barth airfield camp came as a shock. Luftwaffe personnel on the air base must have been well aware of what was going on—the nauseating stench reached one outside the prison fencing. Such inhumanity certainly hardened attitudes toward the Germans among members of our ex-kriegie community.

Sadly, none of the hospitalized concentration camp victims survived despite the efforts of our overworked medics. We still had about 100 patients in our own hospital and no praise is too high for Hankey, Nichols, and the other doctors. With only a few orderlies to help, their dedication under difficult conditions had saved many kriegie lives in the months gone by.

Zhovanik approved of our assistance at the concentration camp and also ordered medical aid for another where conditions were not so bad. Our doctors were already overloaded with work and could not reasonably be expected to do more. Further contact with Zhovanik reinforced my appreciation of the man. He was meeting most of our requests and proved as good as his word. We received vehicles in lieu of those confiscated by his troops, and to meet another of our needs 21 beef cattle and 21 milk cows were rounded up from the local farms. It was like a western cattle drive when these came rushing through the main gate past ranks of yelping ex-kriegies and onto the far end of the peninsula. Here we established a farm under the expert eye of Lieutenant Carl Nelson with our own slaughterhouse and butchery. The big problem was watering these animals. There was plenty of grazing.

In return we had expertise that was currently not available to the

Russians. They appeared to lack competent motor mechanics, and our engineering enthusiasts soon found themselves carrying out repairs on an increasing number of Soviet light vehicles. Zhovanik was impressed by the work Wing Commander J. R. Blackburn's communications team did in resurrecting the local telephone system, as well as the work of our electricians under Squadron Leader Ritchie who helped with the provision of power to the Soviet headquarters.

A message from Zhovanik early the next day informed us that his immediate superior, Major General V. A. Borisov, would be visiting us in two hours. In haste a guard of honor was again assembled and all the camp warned to be on best behavior. Borisov was found to be a far less personable individual than Zhovanik; much more guarded and reticent— more like the Soviet officers I had encountered in 1941. He gave the impression of framing all his statements to conform with Soviet doctrines, as if a political officer was at hand who might report any divergence from the party line. He was amiable while maintaining a formal stance.

Borisov said that until his men had consolidated their positions he would be too busy to be involved in arrangements for our evacuation. The general confirmed that the British and Canadian advance had stopped at Wismar on the Elbe river, just 70 miles from Barth. He forbade us to use our radio transmitter, but had no objection to messages being sent by courier. He also agreed for four Wing X senior officers to travel to the British lines to report to the authorities on the situation in our camp. Borisov went on to thank us for the intelligence provided about SS troops to the west. Then he made a request that really caught me off guard. The bypassed island of Rügen, north of Stralsund, had a garrison of SS troops who were expected to put up a last-ditch stand to cover a V-weapon test site. As his forces were now overstretched, would we provide men to participate in an assault? Tact was essential in my reply: while we would willingly provide a contingent to carry out support activities, our people were nearly all fliers, quite untrained for infantry duties. The question of the language barrier was also pointed out. In my reply care was taken to appear eager to help without making a commitment I knew I had no right to do. Borisov did not pursue the matter and, to my relief, moved on to other topics.

From the contents of Red Cross parcels our cooks did wonders in providing a meal for these important guests. Peanut butter, spam, sardines, and other foods, which were probably strange but hopefully delicacies to the Russian palate. We could not, of course, provide liquor, but the Russians seemed to appreciate our hospitality. Zhovanik, presumably as a result of our talk after the Cossack incident, brought along and presented a number of sidearms for our staff, from which I selected a 9 mm Luger. In another gesture of friendship, the Soviets presented me, as the Senior Allied Officer, with a beautiful dappled white stallion complete with saddle. Youthful experience with pack animals had left me with no love of horses. It was, however, necessary to demonstrate my pleasure by mounting the animal and riding round before the assembly. Where our allies had acquired this beautiful creature I knew not. It had evidently been well ridden for its shoes were all but worn out. With thanks to the general, I had the horse led away to our farm to recuperate. I have never ridden a horse since that day.

Before Borisov departed he invited me and the Wing staff to a celebration that evening at his headquarters, which was in a large house west of Barth. In accepting, I knew what to expect; all attending were warned to refrain from heavy drinking if at all possible and secondly to stay clear of any discussion on subjects that might be disagreeable to our hosts. We all survived pretty well despite the constant drinking of toasts. No sips; our hosts demanded the fiery contents of the glass be tipped down the hatch in one swift gulp.

The following morning a letter was delivered to me from Zhovanik's office. It was a Russian pass together with an English translation. To my astonishment it stated that the bearer, the Senior Allied Officer, was granted permission by the Soviet occupying power to do whatever he wanted in the Barth area. Literally a license to loot, shoot, or what I desired. There was never cause to use it but in dark moments I derived some amusement from speculating on how it could have been employed.

Of mounting concern was the lack of any firm information on what plans, if any, were being developed for our evacuation. Morale had taken a definite downturn and, with news of the British lines so near, numerous people were disobeying orders to stay put and making their own way west on foot. During our meeting with General Borisov the previous day, he had mentioned an agreement between the Soviet and western Allies that liberated POWs would be sent by train to the port of Odessa on the Black Sea. The rail transport of 9,000 ex-kriegies over a vast distance did not bear thinking about and was ridiculous when the British lines were so close. Wing X staff backed me in proclaiming air as our best and quickest means of deliverance. In an effort to expedite matters it was agreed I write a letter to General Spaatz and another to Marshal Rokosoffski of the Red Army, gently suggesting our evacuation by air from the Barth airfield. A letter in similar vein was penned by Group Captain Weir to the British Army commander nearest us. To carry the letters to the west we arranged for Flight Lieutenant William Pickens, an American who served with the Royal Canadian Air Force, to act as courier. Group Captain Hilton and Colonel Byerly would travel with him in the commandeered German vehicles. The Russians agreed to provide an escort.

Later the same day a Jeep with a British army officer and a Russian-speaking NCO arrived from Wismar. The Jeep party had been sent to make contact with our camp and when they returned that afternoon, David Marwood-Elton went with them to reinforce our desire for speedy evacuation.

Meanwhile we had to do our best to keep the ex-kriegies busy or entertained. A very difficult task as the majority became increasingly listless; the one obsession was to go home. People were no longer interested in sport or educational pursuit. We put out popular music on the camp loudspeaker system to try and ease tensions. Russian help was enlisted to lay on one of their renowned song and dance shows during the evening of 7 May. Around a couple of thousand ex-kriegies cheered and applauded a marvelous rendering of Russian ballads and patriotic choruses, no matter that we didn't understand a word. The troupe included a few girls who were probably a little unnerved by the exclamations and wolf whistles when they performed their vigorous twirling dances that exposed a reasonably shapely leg or two. There was little we could do to endorse our thanks for such enjoyable entertainment other than dole out a chocolate bar to each performer.

In a further effort to provide relief to our people, we obtained permission from the Russians to organize marching parties to go sightseeing in the Barth area. Daily passes were issued for single groups of up to 250 men, and the route for most was down to the airfield and back. Unfortunately, once clear of the gates several people broke ranks and wound up in the countryside to do their own exploring. Most eventually returned to camp, although we heard of two who had lodgings with a farming family and were taking out Red Cross food to feed them!

As I had half anticipated, some men who had broken camp got into serious trouble. The Russians found one ex-POW dead in a ditch and another with his head stove in near Barth; most probably murdered by Germans who saw a last chance of revenge on "Terrorfliegers." The bodies were returned and given proper military burial. All the next-of-kin ever knew was that these men died on active service. It depressed me that officers who had survived battle and imprisonment should now throw their lives away by ignoring restrictions. How many others met a similar fate was never brought to light. Several, I expect.

Officially, 8 May 1945 was proclaimed as VE Day—Victory in Europe Day. The most welcome event was the return of Flight Lieutenant Pickens, our courier, in a Jeep with two British soldiers of the 6th Airborne Division. He had been taken to see a British general in Lübeck to whom he passed all the information he could about our camp. This was then supposedly passed up the chain of command to Field Marshal Montgomery who then brought the matter of our evacuation up at a conference with Marshal Rokosoffski. The Soviet marshal had promised that all 9,000 men from Stalag Luft I would be delivered to the British at Wismar within two days. Pickens also informed me that Byerly and Hilton had been flown to England.

In the cause of calming restless souls, I made Pickens's report available for all personnel to see. The troubling fact was that, despite the Soviet promise, absolutely nothing had been heard of this move by their local commanders. As the airborne soldiers and their jeep had to return, I told Pickens to go back as well, explain to the British that we were still waiting, and find out what was happening. Understandably our situation was a low priority in the scheme of things. What concerned me was that we still had not received authoritative news of plans for our evacuation.

Major General Borisov laid on another party that evening to which my staff were invited. In view of Pickens's report that arrangements were in hand by Russian headquarters to evacuate us by road, I took the opportunity to suggest such an exit to Zhovanik. If transport could be found for the sick, the able-bodied should be capable of plodding the 70 miles to Wismar in three or four days. Zhovanik agreed it made sense, so together we put the idea to Borisov. Here my hopes were dashed, for the general was immediately much perturbed that we should wish to take the initiative. The little Russian I could understand was not necessary to realize that Borisov was reprimanding Zhovanik for entertaining the idea, and they were fierce words too. Any such permission had to come from Moscow.

Driving back to camp that night we could see many pyrotechnics arcing into the sky over the airfield. All sorts of ordnance was being discharged, even Teller mines, judging by the loud crumps. Considering the occasion I turned a blind eye to all this, and in any case I was in too much of an alcohol-induced carefree state of mind myself to spoil the other ex-kriegies' fun. Nevertheless, it was with relief I learned next morning that no one had seriously injured or killed himself in playing with explosives.

I was sitting in my office when told Mark Hubbard wanted urgently to speak to me. What I heard was intriguing to say the least: "Hub, you're never going to believe this. I've just seen von Miller among the new German administration the Russians are introducing to the people today. Suggest you get down there right away." It did take some believing. Surely Major von Miller, head of the Abwehr at Stalag Luft I, the kriegies' most despised man, would not have the audacity to show his head round here again. He had been seen in civilian clothes, riding a cycle, on a couple of occasions after von Warnstedt's men left. We imagined he had since fled west.

Arriving in Barth to find the town square crowded with people, Weir and I pushed our way through the throng to where we had arranged to meet Hubbard. In the square a stage had been erected and among the Russian officers and members of the town's new administration was a face I had last seen scowling at me in Stalag Luft I. Gone was military uniform; in its place a neat civilian suit and broad-brimmed grey hat. This chameleon now mixed agreeably with his arch-enemies, the dreaded Bolshevik hordes. The occasion was to celebrate a return to peace, to introduce the new burgomaster and make known the Russian regulations.

Most of the crowd were Pomeranian refugees who had fled to Barth from places further east. Occasionally when one of the speakers on the stage praised the Soviets or denounced the Nazis they were applauded. Amazing! Was this the Master Race? Saving your skin was one thing; to ingratiate to this extent, pathetic. A German read the Russian commander's speech, which displayed a fair and tolerant attitude from the victor and expressed a determination to reestablish a normal situation. Other civilians expressed relief that the war was over, yet from their attitudes they sounded more like speakers for a liberated nation than one soundly defeated. To make us even more incredulous over von Miller's volte-face, one spokesman revealed that the major had met the Red Army outside the town carrying a white flag as acting town policeman. I had heard enough. What position von Miller had obtained in the new administration was not known, but I was determined to see he did not hold it for very much longer. We made our way to Zhovanik's headquarters where the background of this man was given, with a request for his detention.

Back in the square we stood and watched the proceedings. Eventually a Soviet officer approached von Miller, quietly tapped him on the shoulder and beckoned him to follow. That was the last I ever saw or heard of von Miller zu Aichholz. As was their way, the Russians seemed disinclined to detail individual fates. I thought it best not to push the point.

By this date the Russians were getting their act together. The anarchy of the first few days of their presence, with roving groups of Soviet soldiers appearing to do anything that took their fancy, had given way to reasonable order as Zhovanik's control took hold. To assist them, my policy had been to get our people to stay out of their way and abide by their laws. Regrettably, many of the ex-kriegies didn't want to abide by any laws and we received an increasing number of complaints about their activities in the Barth area. Every American or British airman without a pass ended up in the Russian jailhouse. Those who had imbibed too much and objected found rough treatment. No less than 70 of these wayward types were turned over to us by the Russians on 9 May. To pacify the Russians, all marching parties were stopped the following day. Most embarrassingly for me, a head count revealed that of 7,725 Americans in the camp at the time of our taking over from the Luftwaffe, 730 were currently absent; whereas of 1,458 British and Commonwealth men, only 31 could not be accounted for. The RAF, who acted like fools and maniacs at parties and had always been in the forefront of escape efforts, were proving to be the most disciplined in this situation. Perhaps it had something to do with national attitudes that so many Americans had to go roaming the countryside. My concern was not only that they were making trouble with the Russians, but causing friction with the British personnel who felt that so many Americans breaking bounds were laying themselves open to disease and infection and could well start an epidemic when they eventually returned to camp.

It transpired that the majority of the missing men had decided to make their own way home, setting off to walk to the British lines. Nothing short of news of imminent evacuation would curb the unauthorized exodus from the camp. Languishing in a prison area after liberation heightened tensions, and the impatience of the multitude became more evident with each passing day. Whoever had our evacuation in hand obviously didn't appreciate the morale situation. Military bureaucracy was suspected as playing the major part in the delay.

At six in the evening my hopes of good news rose when Pickens returned again, this time in a US Jeep with two American officers. On

reaching the British lines he had been flown to 2nd Army headquarters
at Lüneburg, where the officer in charge of POW repatriation produced
a signal stating that the US XVIII Airborne Corps had been given the
task of organizing air transport to fly us out. Pickens then made his way
to Hagenau, the headquarters of this outfit, only to learn they had received no such signal and that in any case the Russians had not given
permission for aircraft to fly into their zone.

The only glimmer of encouragement in all this was confirmation of the
intention to move us by air, the method we had proposed from the outset
of liberation. Otherwise, Pickens's report simply increased our frustration. It was too much for Ginger Weir who, with a few testy comments
about the incompetency of headquarters staff, demanded that he go and
see Colonel General Pavel Batov, commander of the 65th Soviet Army
that controlled the area, to obtain the permission and then to go to the
Allied lines where, if necessary, he would use rank to get to Montgomery
himself. Certainly we had to try and use rank to get positive action so,
with my blessing, off Weir sped.

Group Captain Weir was as good as his word. At 1830 hours on 11
May we received a report from him via Batov's headquarters at Tribses,
a small town located about 25 miles south of Barth. Batov had cleared the
use of aircraft with Moscow, providing notification of route and times
were agreed beforehand. Ginger was on his way to Hagenau to arrange
the air transport. We passed this news to our people as quickly as possible.

Late that night a tired but jubilant Weir arrived back in camp. Word
had passed to Montgomery who had cleared the air evacuation with
Marshal Rokosoffski. We could expect the first air transports tomorrow.
As word spread through the camp morale took a 100 percent boost.
Mindful of previous disappointments, I just prayed there was no foul-up
this time or that the Soviets didn't change their minds. The Russian
officers who went with Weir to Hagenau to arrange the air evacuation
had signed an agreement allowing a 20-kilometer-wide corridor between
Wismar and Barth to be available on 12 and 13 May between specified
times. Even so, a letter was written to General Batov informing him of

the arrangements and thanking him for his assistance. We planned that
this letter would not be delivered until the first evacuation aircraft were
due to arrive; it would then be too late to rescind the agreement. The
Soviets supplied two release forms for every man in the camp, one in
English and the other in Russian, which kept a team of American-
British-USSR clerks busy for two days.

The first people to go would be the hospital cases, and Lieutenant
Colonel Hankey was alerted to prepare movement. He was also involved
in our subterfuge to honor a promise to three German women who had
aided the POW cause. These had been secretaries in von Warnstedt's
headquarters who supplied information to McCollom's intelligence people in return for a guarantee of safe passage to the west. After the
Luftwaffe staff had left, Hankey put these women to work nursing
concentration camp victims. The plan was to dress them in nurses'
uniforms—hastily run up by the men who made the camp theatrical
gear—and put them on the aircraft flying out the sick and wounded.

Just before 1400 hours on the twelfth, a familiar sound was heard and
a cheer went up from the camp. For there, sweeping low with landing
gear extended, was a B-17—a wonderful sight. At the airfield I found
Brigadier General William Gross, commander of 8th Air Force's 1st Air
Division, an officer I'd last seen at some fighter-bomber critique back in
England, perhaps a year ago. "Well Hub, are you and your boys ready to
move?" he posed. "General, we've been ready for months; what's been
keeping you?" I chided.

Two other B-17s and a C-46 had followed Gross's aircraft into the
field. The B-17s carried radio operators who set up their equipment to
establish a control link with England and 36 more B-17s expected to land
later in the afternoon. The C-46 carried a party from SHAEF (Supreme
Headquarters Allied Expeditionary Forces) headed by Major General
David M. Schlatter, US air officer on Eisenhower's staff who, it transpired, was in overall charge of matters relating to USAAF prisoners of
war. He seemed impressed by our organization and control of the situation. After introduction to Zhovanik, who took Gross and Schlatter off
to meet Borisov, I excused myself as there was much to do in camp.

It was extraordinary how attitudes changed and goodwill blossomed among the ex-kriegies. Campfire barbecues and group singing went on far into the night. Most were too excited by the prospect of departure to get much sleep.

Next day the greater proportion of the former inmates of Stalag Luft I departed, a total of 6,250. Out of the west came a stream of B-17s sweeping down one after the other, some not even cutting all engines while 25 to 30 ex-POWs piled on board. I had decided the British should be the first to leave as among their ranks were several men who had been POWs since before the US came into the war. Just about all the remaining RAF chaps went this day and Ginger Weir in the last B-17 bound for England, with a request to be deposited at his old base at Fulbeck. "Goodbye you rabble-rousing bomber type. Now we fighter boys have finally got the office to ourselves!" He laughed at my facetiousness, clasped hands and said a final "Cheers, Hub." I last saw the lean Ginger Weir headed up the fuselage of the B-17 toward the cockpit. I'll lay odds on that he had charmed his way into the copilot's seat and was flying the ship before they reached England.

A message had come in that six C-46 transports would be arriving mid-morning to take the sick and wounded. Sure enough these big lumbering birds were soon filling our sky as they turned in for final approach, a heart-lifting sight to all of us former birdmen, even though it would not be our turn to go this day. A surprise was the sight of American flight nurses on some of these planes. I don't think these girls could ever have received so many wolf whistles and calls as they did at Barth. In all, 46 C-46s were loaded and took off for France or England. Hankey had managed to get the German girls aboard without any challenge from the watching Russians, who probably thought they were flight nurses.

By the morning of the fourteenth the remaining ex-kriegies were champing at the bit in anticipation, waiting for the deep roar of the B-17s. Soon the long string of big birds could be seen descending to land at Barth. Times were staggered so as not to overload the checking arrangements. As on the previous days the occupants of each barracks had been assembled in the camp and marched out to the airfield in good time.

Most sang as they went; an exuberant chorus of "I've Got Sixpence" rang out across that sad land. By midmorning we last remaining members of Wing X staff had packed our belongings in a pillow case or Red Cross box and assembled at the airfield. The command—if ever it could be called such—was fast evaporating before my eyes. The facilities and accoutrements of Stalag Luft I, including 45,000 Red Cross parcels, had been signed over in total to Major General Borisov on the previous evening. In an expression of gratitude to our Soviet liberators the YMCA band equipment had been handed out piecemeal as gifts to individual soldiers. To Major Svintsov, the officer who had been sent to the camp as the result of the first contact with our scouts, I made a particular point of giving our accordion. Having listened to his rendering of "Three happy tankers, the crew of a fighting machine" and other Soviet war songs after evening dinners, I wanted to make sure higher authority did not appropriate the gift. I had one of our metal workers fix and inscribe a plate stating that it was a personal gift from Colonel Zemke to Major Svintsov "which everyone may use but no one can take away from him."

By 1400 hours only Gross's B-17 remained on the field, the rest of the air fleet having departed. Final good wishes to Borisov, Zhovanik, and the other Soviets were said and it was time to go. In an effort to promote morale I had long told the camp population I would be the last man to leave. Promise fulfilled; the last of 8,498 former POWs to climb through the fuselage door of a B-17 was the one-time Senior Allied Officer.

I have never been a man to carry sentiment for places that have featured large in my life. Yet I will never forget the last view of what was Stalag Luft I: the gate wide, the weather-beaten wood buildings gaunt and silent, no wisps of smoke, no kriegies pounding round the inner boundary wire. Such stark contrast to days just gone when the place teemed with activity. That said, of all my wartime haunts, it is the one I never wish to see again.

9

Operation Flashbowl

The B-17 took off and with one wide sweep of the Barth airfield set course west. A last glance down at the wooden buildings that had constituted Stalag Luft I, and our interest turned to the war-ravaged countryside below. We flew at around 3,000 feet along the north German coast and across the Danish peninsula, before turning southwest. Evidence of Allied bombing was to be seen in most towns and cities we passed over, places once ringed with flak defenses that I had last viewed from the safety of perhaps 25,000 feet. Eventually we crossed into France and were soon on approach to Orly airfield at Paris. Our destination was arranged so that Russ Spicer, Gabby, and myself could be delivered to General Carl Spaatz's headquarters, United States Strategic Air Forces in Europe (USSTAF), which had moved from London to a chateau estate at St.-Germain-en-Laye near Paris. Our presence had been requested in order that we might be debriefed on our experiences, primarily those concerning the administration of Stalag Luft I.

A first move was to discard the assortment of clothing worn in prison camp and draw new army battle fatigues. With these and a fresh haircut we upgraded ourselves to acceptable officer appearance. Apart from being a little thinner and having a more worldly outlook, we had been changed very little by the rigors of prison life. In fact, I surprised myself at how readily and quickly military life was again embraced. Perhaps this was due to my former position as Senior Allied Officer at Stalag Luft I, where the administrative burden and complexity of problems made the position quite as demanding as running a combat group. This resulted in my not being troubled with the tedium suffered by most kriegies, which usually provoked an obsessional desire to be done with the military as soon as possible. All the same, like Spicer and Gabby I was anxious to go back to the States and then catch a piece of the action in the Pacific against the Japanese. However, the local air force chiefs had other ideas.

Evidently General Schlatter had decided that my concern for the well-being of Stalag Luft I prisoners, together with the good rapport we had with the Soviets, made me an ideal candidate for a job he had in mind. This was the location of the 600–700 USAAF prisoners still unaccounted for in the chaos of Germany's unconditional surrender. Most were suspected of having tried to make their own way to Allied lines and been detained by the Russians. Others had probably been killed by revengeful Germans. I was asked to remain in Europe for a few weeks to ferret out these missing POWs. The way it was put to me was that I would have a roving brief throughout Germany. It sounded an interesting task and in any case the request for my services was tantamount to an order. I was to report to SHAEF Headquarters next day. There was to be no leave in which to recover from the rigors of captivity, such was the urgency of the task—or so it appeared.

With the little time left at USSTAF I relished the fine meals and familiar atmosphere of an American military establishment. The glitter of Paris was not an enticement, although I had to make a trip to the base exchange to purchase a razor and other personal requisites. Someone suggested that while in the city I should visit the USAAF Exposition under the Eiffel Tower. This was a public relations exercise for the French, to show them what we had achieved with air power. A number of different types of American warplanes had been trucked to the site and reassembled, including big fellows like the B-17 and B-24. To my surprise, the P-47 on show had been contributed by the 56th Fighter Group and displayed the famous scarlet noseband. I was even more surprised—and greatly moved—when making closer inspection. My old combat command had specially painted up the Thunderbolt with my identification letters, UN-Z, and emblazoned across the fuselage was the legend "Zemke's Wolfpack." It was a fine compliment I didn't deserve.

Next morning I departed Orly for the forward headquarters of SHAEF at Frankfurt-am-Main. General Spaatz's personal pilot, flying the liaison plane, proved to be Joe Clemoe, a close college friend of mine in my Montana forestry days. A small world indeed that two erstwhile buddies should suddenly meet again halfway round the world.

Major Clemoe deposited me at Rhein Main airfield and army ground transport made delivery to Eisenhower's headquarters located in the I. G. Farben Corporation administrative buildings. The Allies, having requisitioned the office complex and surrounding apartments, already had a considerable staff installed, whose immediate task was unraveling the collapsed German economy. Here, reporting to Major General David Schlatter, I was assigned to the office of his assistant, Brigadier General Herbert Thatcher. Of concern was the news that these officers handled a range of air force matters and that the function of recovering former POWs was just one responsibility among many.

I had met Thatcher two years previous, when he had commanded a B-26 Marauder group my fighters had occasionally been called on to escort. A level-headed West Pointer, Thatcher had been promoted after completing his combat tour and appointed to a staff position in the 9th Air Force. The first days of peace in Europe found him again pushed to a SHAEF desk diligently sorting out the never-ending complicities of, mostly it seemed, supply and personnel. Thatcher's energy and inherent administrative ability measurably enhanced the frustration of Zemke, the world's worst staff officer.

There was no time to settle in before I was asked to accompany Major General Schlatter and a sizable number of SHAEF officers to a conference with the Soviets in their occupied zone. The supposed purpose of the meeting was to arrange and coordinate the return of prisoners and displaced persons. Armed with an attache case filled with shorthand scratch pads and an assortment of freshly sharpened pencils, I was ready for action. As it turned out, I could have left all at home and relied on the back of my hand to record the data presented. The venue was a former Luftwaffe base near Halle and our hosts, in jovial mood following their well-earned victory, laid on red carpet treatment for the visiting Allies. Following a short morning meeting where an agenda was drawn up, we adjourned for a scrumptious lunch that would have done justice to the best connoisseur of Paris cuisine. A host of delicacies and choice wines filled the table. Decanters of vodka signaled the inevitable toasts preceding the meal, and this firewater loosened formality in short order. As a result, more than a few of our people were not feeling their best when the afternoon meeting commenced at 1500 hours.

The principal subject for discussion was the imposing problem of the million or so stranded forced laborers brought in by the Germans to keep their war machine going. However, it was soon evident that the Russians' concern lay principally with the rounding up and return of their own subjects who were suspected of defecting to the enemy. Viewed as traitors, these people would either be shot or disappear into the harsh Siberian labor camps. From what had been learned after the liberation of Stalag Luft I, the Soviets had a low opinion of any of their military who allowed themselves to be captured and one wondered just how ordinary prisoners would fare on return to their homeland. Little discussion centered on the western Allied POWs still unaccounted for. Apart from agreeing to abandon the return of our people through Odessa in favor of exchanges across the occupied zone boundaries, few other matters concerning former POWs were touched on. I found that I had no role in this meeting and remained only as a witness.

That evening our hosts staged a lavish banquet in the main dining hall of this former Luftwaffe station. The place was filled with around 150 senior officers resplendent in colored braid and dazzling displays of medal ribbons. Dressed in a plain olive-drab Eisenhower combat jacket and shiny field boots, my status was taken to be that of aide-de-camp brought along to carry the general's baggage; a part happily played, for in the background I could more easily refrain from participating in the continued toasting that was a feature of all Soviet hospitality. General Schlatter, being a very temperate and conservative type, managed to excuse himself soon after dining, which also enabled me to slip away before the vodka flowed too freely.

On return to Frankfurt it was soon apparent that I was henceforth expected to work at a desk. On accepting the assignment I had imagined myself sleuthing round the German countryside in search of missing POWs. Instead, my duties would, for the most part, confine me to this headquarters and, as far as I could see, would simply involve refining and speeding up the process of dealing with the newly found ex-prisoners. The necessary procedures and communication channels having been established prior to my appearance on the scene, it did not take more than a day or two for me to realize that the paperwork involved could quite easily be handled by Thatcher's competent secretary. In fact, I was pretty well superfluous to the whole operation and began to envy the other ex-POWs from Barth who had been flown to Rheims to await sea passage to the States from Le Havre.

For the time being there were pressing personal matters that had to be resolved. As I had arrived at this assignment without written orders, records, or identification, the Army would not accept any claims for pay and subsistence. Although I was credited with several months' back pay, the appropriate authority was as yet not forthcoming with the necessary paperwork, forcing me to write a few IOUs with long-time associates in order to pick up a couple of hundred dollars and avoid being completely destitute. Also lacking was an official Army identification card, making any venture outside the I. G. Farben complex a risky undertaking. If challenged, failure to establish identity could lead to incarceration in a local guardhouse until a ranking associate could be found to bail me out. So, at first, it was prudent to remain in the headquarters and my own room situated in the same complex.

Every morning teletype messages came from Allied units providing the names and dispositions of ex-POWs who had turned up. Somewhat surprising were the places where these people had surfaced. Cannes, Paris, Rome, Switzerland, England, and even two in Cairo! It appeared they were intent on having a good time and for various reasons were happy to be listed as missing. Once I had read the morning reports and perhaps drafted a few papers, it was a matter of leaning back in my swivel chair to kill time. After devoting some study and thought to the flying and alighting skills of the housefly, even the lack of an identity card could not contain my wishes to escape from the office and seek more demanding activity. A request was made to Thatcher that I be allowed to visit Rhein Main airfield and catch up on missed flying hours. This granted, no time was lost in obtaining transport and seeking the flight line serving the SHAEF headquarters. To my delight, among a line of liaison and light transport aircraft sat a few war-weary P-47s. These, it was later learned, were ostensibly for staff courier service but in truth were retained through the whim of a few officers who wanted to indulge themselves in pushing a powerful fighter around the heavens while qualifying for flight pay.

Entering the tent which served as an operations office, I found a sergeant at a desk. My request to fly one of his P-47s that afternoon was met with a courteous enquiry as to who had granted the authority. Without my flight records and orders, it developed he could do little for me; after some fruitless discussion I resorted to rank. Would he get the base commander on the phone so that I could speak to him and resolve this impasse? At first the sergeant tried to persuade me to talk to his operations officer; I assured the sergeant that this was not an attempt to get him into hot water, but that I was determined to fly that afternoon. I simply wanted to explain matters to the base commander. The base commander was out, but his secretary said she would call back when he returned.

To idle my time away I walked to the parked aircraft to look them over and assess their condition. In due time the sergeant came out to tell me the base commander was in and ready to receive my call. Here too my request was not well received, and realizing I was getting nowhere fast I asked if he would do me a favor and call General Thatcher's office to confirm my need as genuine. Pending the result of this further try I ambled out onto the field again. Soon afterward the sergeant came running to inform me that the base commander had just called to say I had permission to fly anything I wanted and that a P-47 would be made ready for me as soon as possible. What Thatcher had said I never learned, but the episode was a prime example of "it's who you know that counts." Nevertheless I was mindful that had he not been in his office my endeavors to fly would have failed, and that lacking an identity card my position could have been precarious.

The perseverance was well worth while in view of the challenge and pleasure of taking a P-47 into the air after eight months' absence from a fighter cockpit. An hour or so's flight round the Frankfurt area only strengthened my desire to get back to a flying assignment at the first opportunity. After landing back at Rhein Main and nursing a bit of self-satisfaction that I could still master the brute, I returned to SHAEF headquarters. Alas, my troubles were not yet over. Lacking identification, I was barred from entering by the guards, and only after the duty officer in my department presented himself at the front gate to vouch for me was entry permitted. Until those papers were received I was to some extent still a prisoner.

My frustration with the assignment increased with each passing day, even though it was supposed to be only temporary. A good secretary could still do my work in the time it took for her coffee break; in fact Thatcher's did handle most of my paperwork. Bored, I was frequently mentioning my desire to get back to being a fighter pilot to both Thatcher and Schlatter, more to emphasize that I was not cut out for staff work than with any hope of relief. Perhaps someone in General Spaatz's headquarters had thought this job was good therapy for a former prisoner, but, having spent most of my service life carefully avoiding staff posts, the concern now was not to get trapped in the military paper-pushing world.

At last, in receipt of identification papers, I could at least venture out from the SHAEF building without fear of falling under arrest. Rhein Main airfield and flying the staff aircraft were the usual attraction. While there I heard a rumor that a cache of six Luftwaffe Fieseler Storchs had been seen on a farm near Giebelstadt. The Storch was a single-engine high wing monoplane that we would classify as a liaison type. The Luftwaffe had used them extensively for such duties as well as for observation. They were said to have remarkable short landing and takeoff capability. As one of my informants gave quite clear details of where these aircraft were supposedly located, I decided to investigate at an early opportunity.

With the benefit of rank, a vehicle and the services of a flight mechanic were obtained. Several cans of aviation gasoline and a small drum of oil were loaded and off we went. Rumor was rife in Germany during these early postwar days and I expected this one, like most, would turn out to be false. Much to my delight it proved to be true. Locating the farm, we found five Storchs tucked away in the barn and a sixth outside, covered with a tarpaulin. The farmer was informed these military aircraft were being confiscated by the US Army. If the farmer knew why these planes had been stashed away here, he wasn't telling, but I suspect either they had featured in some last-minute escape plan or an optimistic Luftwaffe officer hoped the day would dawn when he could make a pretty Deutschemark. The decision was made to try and fly the Storch under the tarpaulin. Having no technical manuals to rely on, the sergeant and I looked the aircraft over as best we could, determining that they hadn't been booby-trapped and were safe for flying. The problem for me was to calculate the operating limits, as the gauges were all calibrated in the metric system. Having made my judgments, I marked the instruments with green paint to simplify reading them. As a favorite trick of the Germans, when abandoning aircraft, was to put sand in the fuel and oil tanks, all were drained, purged, and refueled. All preflight work performed, the time came to try and start the beast. Much to our surprise, after a single fuel priming the engine broke into life at the first attempt. Not wanting to jeopardize the life of the sergeant, I instructed him to drive the car back to base. Taxiing out onto a fairly large grass field near the barn, the Storch was headed into wind and the throttle pushed wide open. The beastie virtually bounded into the air. A few circuits proved it was a little dreamship to fly and almost impossible to stall. The large amount of glazing around the cockpit allowed an exceptional downward view on each side. Arriving at Rhein Main, I found the Storch glided in like a homing pigeon and landed safely below the speed I'd calculated.

In due course the other five aircraft were dusted down and flown to Rhein Main. US stars and bars were painted over the original crosses and the six machines tethered near Operations in a neat line where they soon became known as "Zemke's Air Force." Few if any other pilots in Europe had the luxury of their own personal air transport with five spares. I suspect my activities in liberating these aircraft were not altogether viewed with approval by some senior officers but tolerated as activity expected of a frustrated fighter type.

My work taking progressively fewer hours each day, I decided to expand my personal reparations, currently consisting of the Luger pistol presented by Colonel Zhovanik and six Fieseler Storchs. The Germans had a worldwide reputation for high-quality cameras, and it was learned that the famous Leica was still in production. During my stay at Dulag-Luft, I had often viewed the Leica plant at nearby Wetzlar; now a trip was made in the Storch. Arriving at the plant, I found it surrounded and heavily guarded by US Army police. An attempt to gain access was firmly rejected, rank being of no advantage. In response to an enquiry about the availability of cameras, it was made plain that there were none and that my presence was definitely not wanted. This cool reception and the heavy guard suggested that a good number of US and Allied military personnel had also had similar ideas to mine.

Back at SHAEF headquarters I learned that an old friend, Colonel Gilbert Myers, had called and left an invitation to visit him at Erfurt where he was Chief of Staff with the XIX Tactical Air Command. Gil had been in the 8th Pursuit Group at Langley, where he and I were chosen to fly the accelerated service tests on the P-40 at Wright Field in summer 1940. Gil had also been one of the three original officers assigned to the 56th Fighter Group on its formation at Savannah, Georgia, but was transferred out before I arrived. Later he commanded a P-47 OTU in New England and brought the 368th Fighter Group, a 9th Air Force outfit, to England, getting his combat introductory missions with my group at Halesworth. Not having seen him since then, I jumped at the opportunity to visit and hear about "his war." I obtained two days "basket" leave; the Storch was strapped on and flown to Erfurt where Gil picked me up in a staff car and drove me to his quarters in a large house requisitioned for officers of his command. We had a merry time relating our respective experiences. In the course of the evening Myers mentioned that he had recently run across a lieutenant who had served with the 56th Group. This man was presently stationed a few miles away at the Carl Zeiss factory at Jena. The thought that immediately flashed through my mind was Contax, a 35 mm camera for which Zeiss was famous. Gil couldn't recall the man's name, but as I was so interested he would have a member of his staff put in a phone call to the plant next morning. I didn't reveal the ulterior motive for my interest.

The former 56th Group member turned out to be none other than First Lieutenant Irving Brayer, who had been my chief of the photographic section in headquarters. Talking with Brayer over the phone I learned that a single enlisted man and he were in charge of the photographic section of Zeiss works and were more than overwhelmed with problems. Originally the US 1st Army had assigned a small staff headed by a lieutenant colonel to secure the factories, but he had been reassigned and no replacements had been forthcoming. Sympathizing with his predicament, I said I would be right over. He indicated he would be pleased to see me and could use some help and advice. The quest for a camera hadn't been mentioned but I couldn't believe my luck; an entire factory with a lieutenant from my old outfit in charge!

Borrowing a staff car from Gil, I soon covered the few miles to Jena. The Zeiss Optical complex was easy to find and, surprisingly, smoke still issued from the factory stacks. The place appeared to have suffered no air

raid damage during hostilities. It was later learned that only one bombing attack had been made on the plant and that, apparently, inaccurately.
Suffice it to say my first question to Brayer was just how he came to be
here and not with the 56th back in England. His answer was that at the
end of hostilities a certain Colonel George Goddard, concerned with
photographic technology, had received permission to pluck people with
the right qualifications from USAAF units in Europe to form ad hoc
intelligence teams to investigate all aspects of the enemy's photographic
technique, equipment, and manufacture. Somehow, Brayer's part in this
was to find himself on temporary transfer from running the small photo
lab at Boxted, England, to acting as the Allied representative in charge
of one of the foremost optical works in the world. Apart from being
responsible for security, he also had to assist the many visiting technical
teams from the US and UK, processing their requests for equipment and
data. No wonder he felt out of his depth. A ridiculous situation for one
officer when there were thousands of US military personnel just kicking
their heels in Europe who could be brought in to help.

I vaguely recalled Colonel Goddard as the fatherly type I had met
while testing P-40s at Wright Field. As an army scientist in a cloistered
laboratory, working on some intricate problem was his chief interest in
life. It transpired that he was responsible for many important developments in the field of aerial photography. However, if the situation at
Zeiss was his responsibility, then he was not much of a manager.

While acknowledging Brayer's plight and promising to see what I
could do back at SHAEF headquarters, I thought the time was now opportune to voice my desire to obtain a Contax. My balloon was quickly
popped, for Brayer said he could offer field artillery ranging devices,
submarine telescopes, large naval binoculars, laboratory microscopes,
and much specialized optical equipment built at Jena, but not cameras.
They were built by the Zeiss plants in either Berlin or Dresden. Brayer
then invited me to tour the works where, surprisingly, some production
continued, apparently on orders of the Allies. I learned that Zeiss had
several new developments that were of immense interest to the Allied
technical investigation teams. Thanking Brayer and reiterating my inten-

tion of seeing what could be done to help him, I flew back to Frankfurt resolving that while keeping my word I wasn't going to further involve myself.

Military supervision of the Zeiss Optical complex was soon forgotten when on landing at Rhein Main I saw that my five spare Fieseler Storchs had disappeared. The sergeant, who acted as crew chief, explained that they had been given to the French Air Force, whose pilots had flown them away to their base at Lahr. The order had come from high places via the Rhein Main commander. Although I was incensed that this appeared to have been done behind my back, there was nothing more to be said as I had no more right to the aircraft than whoever gave them away. Later in Thatcher's office, a casual remark to the effect that nothing was sacred any more in the service drew the query "How so?" My reply was that some clod had given away my air force of liberated Storchs to the French. Thatcher smiled. "We had complaints from the base commander at Rhein Main that you were dumping a lot of work on his men. As we have more American aircraft scattered around than we can possibly keep in commission, the German aircraft were given to the French in a deal." What the deal was he didn't say and I wasn't going to press the point. From what he had just said it looked as if the decision to give away Zemke's loot had been made at general officer level. There had been no workload on Rhein Main mechanics, in any case there were plenty of them around, so I figured this was just an explanation to feed me. More likely the local USAAF command was anxious to tighten up on the laxness widespread after the end of hostilities and an irregularity that they couldn't live with was this buccaneering fighter colonel setting up his own Luftwaffe.

Remembering my promise to Brayer, I spent the next day or so, all to no avail, trying to discover what section of the giant SHAEF staff was responsible for matters at Zeiss Optical. I spoke to my immediate superiors about this dilemma, and General Schlatter said he would try to find Colonel Goddard, who seemed to be constantly on the move around Europe, and call him in for a review of the situation. By coincidence Goddard happened to turn up in Frankfurt later that week and was snared by Schlatter—they were old buddies from prewar days—for a meeting that I was told to attend. The affable old colonel was every bit what the British termed a "boffin," a scientist absorbed in his subject. He was more intent on describing his discoveries in Germany than discussing the matter I had raised. His current objective was to seek out and secure anything and everything new in the field of photography for the USAAF. Apparently Zeiss had a device that could revolutionize the grinding of optical lenses, superior to anything similar he had seen elsewhere. The company was also way ahead in infrared photography and had developed a special camera and film that could be used to allow a submarine to navigate through dense fog with precision. He rated their Professor Jost one of the top dozen photographic experts in the world. Much of what Goddard said was lost on me as my technical knowledge of photography never got much beyond my boyhood dissection of a Kodak box camera, an act that did not please my parents from whom it had been a gift.

Finally, I was able to ask Goddard why, if the developments at Zeiss were so valuable to our nation, he had only assigned a lieutenant and a sergeant from a fighter unit in England to handle the entire gamut of overseeing activities at Jena. His reply was to the effect that such personnel were all that had been provided and of late he had been too busy traveling around Europe to make better arrangements. And wasn't the Army in control there? Respectfully I told him of my visit and observations at Jena, where Brayer was overloaded with responsibility. Surely he could arrange more assistance for a project of the importance he had indicated?

Having made my points for Brayer I had no intention of contributing more to this meeting, but I was in for a surprise. General Schlatter, who had been listening to all this, turned to me and said, "Zemke, you haven't much work on your hands at the moment. Why don't you go to Jena for a week or two and sort things out. In the meantime I'll try and make arrangements for assistance to expedite George's requirements from Zeiss." Taken aback by this new development and mentally chastising myself for not keeping away from other people's problems, before I realized it the meeting was over with Schlatter and Goddard shaking

hands before parting company. Thatcher probably recognized my dis-
quiet for, grinning, he commented, "You get all the fun!" and then
added, "I could use a Contax camera if you find one."

Next morning I was off to Erfurt with my toothbrush. By now the task
at Jena didn't seem too bad in that it would remove me from the staff
bureaucracy at SHAEF. A telephone call the previous evening had
drawn an invitation from Gil Myers to make his home my quarters. Gil
also obliged by furnishing a staff car to take me the few miles to and from
Jena each day.

Brayer was pleased to see me and, I suspected, relieved to unload the
responsibility of Zeiss Optical onto someone else's shoulders. My first
requirement was an office. Brayer escorted me into a spacious wood-
paneled and Persian-carpeted suite in the main Zeiss building. This had
been provided him by the Zeiss management, but he now said he would
be cozier in an outer office with the sergeant and would turn this opulent
room over to me. I discovered that two other US Army officers were at
Zeiss, a Captain Linder and a Lieutenant Gimsberg, with a vague assignment to oversee matters concerned with the requisition of binoculars.
Nobody had precise written orders, functioning on verbal advice and
assumptions. Now I had to operate in the same way.

My new "command" was more extensive than I had at first appreci-
ated. In addition to the Zeiss plant, my administration extended to the
Schott und Genossen Glas-Werke, one of the foremost manufacturers of
specialist glass. The Zeiss management had, apparently, been exceedingly cooperative, undoubtedly hoping to preserve their industry for
happier times in the future. An advantage for my presence was that I
could converse in German whereas Brayer had to rely on an interpreter,
although several people at Zeiss were fluent in English. My immediate
task was to ensure proper security, particularly against casual British or
American personnel who came looking for loot; notably cameras! Zeiss
had their own security guards who were quite able to deal with their own
countrymen, but knuckled under when anyone in Allied uniform arrived. Next, guidelines for dealing with authorized technical inspection
teams were drawn up to try and effect some control over these frequent

visitors. That evening, back at XIX TAC headquarters, a telephone call was made to General Thatcher giving my requirements. These were notably a full military police company to secure the factory on a 24-hour basis and a half dozen GI trucks with driver to remove requisitioned items to designated locations for shipment to the US or UK. The following day the MPs arrived and were soon positioned to check all who entered or left the factory area. Thatcher also arranged the required transport and for a sub-depot at Hanau to handle all shipments from Zeiss that the technical teams dispatched.

After a week or so the situation appeared to be under control, with security much improved and officially requisitioned items being packed and dispatched as required. In fact all went fairly smoothly until one day when a concerned Colonel Goddard suddenly appeared on the scene. From his attache case he produced maps and papers to support his tale of woe. In an adjustment of occupied zones agreed among the Allies, Jena and the surrounding area were to be turned over to the Soviets. They would have the choice of dismantling any factory in their zone as some amends for the devastation wrought by the Nazi invasion of the Russian homelands. The loss of Jena with its major optical companies would seriously affect production at smaller dependent factories in the British and American zones which relied on Jena for optical components. This was particularly so in the case of Schott, which was responsible for up to 95 percent of molten and crystal glass manufactured in Germany. If the German economy was to be revived it was essential that Zeiss and Schott expertise was retained. The western Allies needed to remove the plant from Jena to a location in our zones where it could be reestablished as a nucleus for future expansion.

Up to this moment it had been my understanding that, to ensure Germany was never again able to rebuild its military might, all industry was to be dismantled. The nation was going to be in the doghouse for years. We were not even supposed to associate with any Germans; a policy of nonfraternization was in force. Now, here I was being told that we were intent on reconstructing the German economy. Goddard, however, was firm in his conviction. He had already earmarked a glass plant near Munich, to which he wanted to transfer certain of the optical manufacturing machinery. A considerable number of engineers and key staff would have to move to form the basis of the new work force.

My reaction was to go into reverse by reminding him that I was a side-tracked fighter pilot who was expecting to be sent home any day now. Notwithstanding my lack of enthusiasm, Goddard asked to see the Zeiss directors on this matter. A meeting with the German board was arranged for that evening. The Zeiss people turned up in force, and with the aid of an interpreter Goddard outlined his plan. No doubt the news came as a great shock but the board were quick to show their support. Like most Germans, they were fearful of what their lot might be under the Russians.

Still somewhat perplexed by this turn of events, on return to XIX TAC headquarters, which had a telephone link with SHAEF, I put a call in to Thatcher to ask what he knew about Goddard's plan to move Zeiss. Thatcher said he had heard something along those lines but suggested I bring Goddard into SHAEF headquarters next day for a meeting with General Schlatter. Having gotten transport from Gil Myers, at 1100 hours on the morrow Goddard and I were in Schlatter's office. From what followed it appeared that Goddard's plan was known and approved in high places. For the first time I learned officially that the Russians were scheduled to take over Jena in three weeks. Everyone else seemed to have been told except me, an infuriating lack of communication but I knew better than to complain. Hopeful that I might now be relieved of my lame-duck duties at Zeiss, instead I was sent back to Jena to await further developments.

It had been determined that the United States would move a key nucleus of the Zeiss work force to Munich, but they also wanted to interrogate a number of the optical experts at a center near Stuttgart. No one knew exactly how many select people were involved or the exact quantity of equipment to be moved. In fact, who was to be in charge of this new enterprise was not clear. While Goddard held forth on the desirability of the transfer, I doubted if he understood the magnitude of what he proposed and its accomplishment in such a short time. Everything seemed rather vague, and while without any precise instruction, I decided to pursue the necessary preliminaries for an exodus.

Back at Jena the next morning, the visiting photographic intelligence personnel were called into my office and told to make haste in completing their projects. Additionally, I asked them to draw up lists of Zeiss and Schott engineers and scientists recommended for further interrogation in the US occupied zone. Then the Zeiss directors were called to a meeting and informed of what had been proposed during my visit to SHAEF.

During the next two days the list of individuals to be moved was finalized at 122, plus dependents, although illness and other circumstances saw continual fluctuation in the total. Of necessity, I had to rely on the competence of the visiting intelligence teams to identify key people, although I had hoped for some guidance from Goddard. However, the Wright Field boffin was off somewhere else and did not appear at Jena again. When the list was presented to them, the Zeiss and Schott people were obviously shocked that the number of people was so small a proportion of the total staff. Several people not on the list later approached me begging to be included, only to be told there could be no expansion of numbers. As it stood, the movement of 122 men and their immediate dependents, plus some personal belongings, was quite an undertaking in the circumstances.

After discussion with Thatcher, the US 7th Army, currently responsible for the area in which Jena was situated, was approached again, this time for the provision of 122 two and a half ton GI trucks with two drivers each. The head of each family was told that once a truck had arrived for him there would be 24 hours to get whatever belongings they had decided to take, and themselves, onto the vehicle. The drivers would assist with loading but there could be no delays.

The next step was to arrange the removal of specialized machinery and other vital equipment from the factory. Again telephoning Thatcher, I made arrangements to assemble a freight train at Jena. To move all equipment the Zeiss staff considered essential would have taken 40 trains, although Thatcher thought 40 freight cars extravagant. Having never seen the plant he didn't realize the size and scope of the place. However, he agreed to arrange for a train. No directives were forthcoming from SHAEF on the evacuation and they were apparently leaving me to my own devices. As the saying goes: "Ever onward and upward."

Meanwhile the adrenalin had really begun to flow at Zeiss. The company worked 24 hours a day feverishly unbolting machine tools from concrete floors, crating instruments, and assembling technical papers. During this time I received a succession of requests and questions. For example, in the case of determining dependents who were to be transported to the western zones, could the father and mother constitute eligible evacuees? Yes, but be certain they are not younger than you, was my answer. Would there be food and rest stops en route? Again my reply was evasive; take what food you think you'll need for 24 hours. I will provide an army C-ration for each truck. The GI drivers will cooperate for rest stops. They are human too, I believe. One selected engineer stated that his wife was pregnant and about to have a baby. Should he take her along or leave her in Jena? My answer, perhaps a bit callous and blunt, was "Mein Herr, the decision rests entirely with you. I can only provide transportation, not medical service. The GI drivers will help but they are not qualified in midwifery."

Then there were complications with the local banks. The departing Zeiss people wanted to withdraw their life savings, even if the Reichmark had little value. Unfortunately for them, private bank accounts had been frozen at the end of hostilities. Strapping on my Luger and taking the list of those to be evacuated, I paid a visit with Brayer to the Jena banks. Taking an authoritative stance, I told each bank manager that as US representative in charge of the Zeiss and Schott plants I was directing him to pay these people whose names appeared on the list what they required from their accounts. Before returning to my office I insisted on overseeing the first few customers paid out. This was accomplished with the usual surfeit of form stamping—endemic in Germany at this time.

A much more interesting problem arrived on my desk one afternoon. Brayer came into my office followed by his German interpreter and excitedly emptied the contents of some small bags before me. "Look what we've unearthed." He was grinning from ear to ear, like a small boy who had just found a full box of candy. I looked at the small heaps of what appeared to be broken quartz. "Industrial diamonds!" Brayer announced triumphantly. Picking up a couple of the larger ones, about the size of small peas, I asked the German how much they were worth. He replied that at current world prices, between $70,000 and $80,000 the pair. For a moment I thought, "Devil, get your hand off my shoulder." Two faces looked down at me expectantly. "Call the Captain of the MP company immediately, Brayer. Then I want you two to count the diamonds and make out a receipt in triplicate, one for Zeiss, one for SHAEF headquarters, and one for me." The diamonds were later conveyed by MPs to US Army headquarters at Erfurt; not without the thought, "Easy come, easy go."

About a week after preparations for the evacuation were set up, Irving Brayer brought the news that a small Soviet advance party had set up residence in one of the local guest houses. Unaware whether the US authorities had made their removal of the cream of the Zeiss establishment known to the Russians, when two Soviet officers arrived at the main gate next day demanding admittance, I decided to take no chances. Telling Brayer to show them into my office, the pet Luger was purposely placed on the desk. Not with hostile intent, but to indicate clearly that this was a military command post. Whatever the purpose of the Soviets' visit, my obligations to them had no bearing upon my present responsibility. I intended to get rid of them and stall. Presently a Red Army colonel and captain entered, the latter proving to be an interpreter. After shaking hands and making introductions, they were invited to sit down. In answer to my opening question as to why they wanted to enter the Carl Zeiss works, they stated they were an advanced echelon from the Red Army conducting a survey of the area that their forces would shortly occupy. This visit was to inspect the factory and talk to the management.

Pausing for a moment to appear as if I was deeply evaluating their request, I then asked, courteously, for credentials, particularly a written letter designating them to reconnoiter the Zeiss factory. They replied that they had none apart from their Soviet identity cards. Continuing in a genial manner, I informed them that much as I would like to meet their request, because of recent intrusions and looting at the factory, I had been issued strict instructions not to permit entry to anyone, Allied or German, without the proper written authority. Thus I could not grant their request at this time. If they obtained the necessary authorization then I would be pleased to give them access. Both Russians looked a trifle dismayed, although I fancied they accepted the situation, which must have been akin to any such approach made to their own authorities had the boot been on the other foot. To underline friendliness I personally escorted them to the main gate and bade them farewell. Nevertheless, I had a hunch their superiors would not be pleased.

That the Russians lost no time in making representations was quickly evident. Next day, 26 June, I received a direct order from SHAEF that any production machinery removed from the factory had to be reinstated and in no time at all two G-4 supply officers from the 7th Army arrived to ensure the work was done without delay. There was no requirement concerning requisitioned equipment. In any case, most had already been dispatched to the US Army Disarmament Depot at Hanau, near Frankfurt. With these consignments had gone unclassified patents, documents, drawings, laboratory equipment, and specialist machinery applicable to all the enterprises at Jena that the Zeiss and Schott people had said should be "saved."

There was now no time to be lost in evacuation of the selected Zeiss and Schott personnel and their dependents. I had received no written orders for their dispatch and put the operation in progress on the strength of the verbal desires of Goddard and my contacts at SHAEF. On 26 and 27 June the fleet of trucks supplied by VI Armored Corps carried out the movement. The total of 435 individuals was made up of 81 Zeiss people with 202 family members, and 43 from Schott plus 109 dependents. Some of the family members looked a bit suspicious to me but there wasn't time for further investigations of legitimacy. What was important was that we had the brains of both businesses and here I don't think there were any slips. Among the many distinguished scientists, the trucks conveyed Doctor Irig Kuppebender, head of the Zeiss operation, plus wife, daughter, son, and adopted son. Also Doctor Erich Schott, president of the German optical glass industries, with wife, son, and mother.

When I arrived back at XIX TAC headquarters next evening, Gil Myers informed me an anxious General Thatcher had been urgently trying to make contact. Using the hot line, I couldn't raise Thatcher and was put onto the SHAEF duty officer. All he knew was that I was to pack my bag and get back to SHAEF HQ as soon as possible.

As directed, the next morning the erstwhile US overseer of Zeiss Optical arrived in his immediate superior's office. Thatcher seemed relieved to see me. The gist of what he then related was that the previous day SHAEF had received a telephone call from the commanding general of the US Air Forces in Europe saying that he wanted Colonel Hubert Zemke out of Germany and on his way back to the US within 48 hours. My name had been mentioned by the Russians at a four-power conference in Berlin, where they were evidently far from happy that the best of Zeiss had been snatched from underneath their noses. Questions were being asked on the Allied side as to just what a fighter pilot was doing in Jena and under whose authorization.

Well, this was good news to me as there was nothing to stop me from leaving right away. There was one request: I would like to drive to Orly Airport in Paris, from which the trans-Atlantic flights departed. During my service in Europe there had been little opportunity to see the French countryside. Thatcher was a little hesitant, but as I'd just handed him a used Contax camera that Brayer's German interpreter had found in Jena town for the equivalent of $16, he mellowed and said he would contact the motor pool. There was a strong warning about breaking down or getting lost en route, for he was not prepared to bail me out with higher authority in the current circumstances.

Having collected the necessary travel permits, I went to my quarters, seldom occupied in the past month, to find there had been a thief around. I assume a German, as none of my papers or military items had gone, only clothing and personal stuff. Throwing what remained into a duffel bag, I made tracks for the motor pool where several confiscated German cars were on hand. Looking these over I selected a black BMW convertible on which US Army insignia and numbers had been painted. To avoid any embarrassment to Thatcher, four full jerry cans of fuel and a couple of extra tires and tubes were stowed aboard before I was on my way across the Rhine and westward. Driving across France in all its summer splendor with the top down and with home as the ultimate destination was an exhilarating experience. Thatcher need not have worried because I made Paris in good time next day, reporting to the US Embassy. The Marine guard at the main desk was taken aback to be asked, "Son, do you want a car? Well, here are the keys, it's yours. You'll find it standing just outside at the curb." From the air attache's office a staff car ride to Orly was obtained.

Before the day was out I was seated in a C-54 transport winging across the Atlantic. A day and a half later found me in Washington, D.C., at the Pentagon. The Air Force was interested in my experiences in Stalag Luft I and for a few days treated me to a number of debriefing sessions. Nothing was ever said about the Carl Zeiss evacuation; presumably this was a business remote from the USAAF in Washington. Unbeknown to me at the time, the episode had nearly caused an international incident, with the Russians making accusations of dirty tricks. In SHAEF questions were being asked about responsibility and a lack of any written authority—I certainly hadn't seen anything on paper. Embarrassingly for SHAEF, it appeared that off-the-cuff support had been accorded the enthusiasms of a Wright Field boffin who had disappeared from the scene at an early date. Attention was then directed to the buccaneering fighter colonel who implemented the evacuation and called the shots at Jena. If not the villain, a convenient scapegoat; and there was I, thousands of miles away, congratulating myself on a fair piece of organization and administration at Jena.

At last it was back home to Montana and my family. Now perhaps the effort of the past few years caught up with me, for I became very tired, a kind of exhaustion. The plan was to get an assignment to the Pacific theater after my leave, but the dropping of the A-bombs changed all that. Japan surrendered and the war was over.

An Epilogue

Colonel Hubert Zemke looked to continue his air force career following a well-earned rest. While the vast majority of American men were eager to return to civilian life following the end of the Second World War, there were several volunteers and conscripts who liked the camaraderie and order of military life and looked to making a peacetime career in one of the services. Unfortunately for these men, such was the scale of ordered demobilization during the first postwar year that the Army and Navy were more intent on shedding personnel than retaining them. Hub, having a permanent commission, was assured of continuing service in the Army Air Forces, albeit his permanent rank was still that of first lieutenant. However, USAAF policy was not to demote career officers but to let them keep their temporary rank until qualifying for this on a permanent basis.

The peacetime USAAF, soon to become the USAF, underwent much readjustment as priorities changed. Many fighter pilots found it very difficult to come to terms with the tempo and restrictions of the peacetime force following their war service, where individual initiative and flight prowess had been openly fostered. Some could never live with the changed circumstances and resigned, particularly where the disciplinarians and sticklers for military protocol had reasserted their presence in command. Among those resigning were numerous distinguished aces.

There was another aspect to furthering a career in fighter aviation. The bomber arm and bomber personnel dominated the scene, primarily because the endeavors to attain autonomy by the Army Air Forces and its forebear had rested on proving the concept of strategic bombing. That goal was finally achieved through the atomic bomb with its awesome destructive power. Initially only aircraft could deliver it, confirming the bomber as the major instrument of deterrence. Thus the bomber camp held sway, and as bomber personnel were the mainstream in the Second World War, they remained far more numerous than fighter men in the postwar force. Bomber generals would, in fact, dominate the command of the USAF for 40 years. Ironically, it had been well proven between 1939 and 1945 that for the bomber to succeed the fighter must first achieve air superiority in the area of offensive operations. Nevertheless, the USAF hierarchy held the bomber to be the foundation of air power and in general the influence of fighter men was limited. A brilliant record as an air ace counted for little in the promotion stakes in the years following the defeat of the Axis powers. Yesterday's heroes were a dime a dozen.

Hub didn't even recognize himself as a hero, but he expected to find a fighter group command as his assignment following a month spent recuperating, mostly on his father's recently acquired ranch in northern Idaho. Instead he was sent to serve as desk-bound executive officer at the Air Proving Grounds, Elgin Field, east of Pensacola, Florida, an establishment involved in testing equipment and developing new operating techniques. This hiving off of such a capable fighter leader was possibly a repercussion of the Zeiss affair: a form of official reprimand. If so, it was an admonishment that Hub thought ill-deserved, in that he appeared to be made the scapegoat for inept administration at high command level.

The posting to Elgin was brief, and in January Hub was given the position as Director of Tactics at the Air Tactical School of the USAAF's Air University at Tyndall Air Base, about 50 miles from Elgin. This assignment was to last three years. While Hub was well qualified for the job of teaching fighter doctrine to students, he was not at his happiest tied to another staff job. There was, however, opportunity to fly combat aircraft. He mastered the technique of handling a new jet, the Lockheed P-80 Shooting Star, which was in production as the first American service jet fighter. Nonetheless, it was somewhat galling to see wartime buddies still furthering their careers in fighters. The 56th Fighter Group was re-formed at Selfridge Field, Michigan, in May 1946 with Dave Schilling (Hub's air executive when commanding that organization) at the helm and other former members among the complement of pilots. Starting out on Mustangs, the group was soon flying Shooting Stars with Schilling leading them in the first Atlantic crossing to Britain by jet formations.

Having reduced the air forces to a state where, as one critic said, they were not strong enough to fight their way out of a paper bag, the United States was gradually forced into rearming. Concern on finding that the Soviets were developing their own strategic forces and the blockade of Berlin in 1948 led to an expansion of the USAF, albeit slowly. In January 1949 Hub received the kind of assignment he had been seeking, to Furstenfeldbruck airfield, near Munich, Germany. Here he commanded the 36th Fighter Group, at the time the only USAF unit in Europe equipped with the P-80 jets. Relations between the Soviets and western nations were at rock bottom; if there was going to be military conflict it looked as if Europe was the place.

A few weeks after Hub assumed command, the German magazine *Stern* ran an article on the Furstenfeldbruck fighter establishment, which stood on alert for any interference with Berlin airlift traffic. Mention was made of the commander's name, which was evidently noted by some of the Zeiss management. They wrote to Hub asking if he would care to visit them at their new plant at Oberkochen, he being partly responsible for the reestablishment of their company in the west. Hub's response was cordial, pleading pressure of work as making him unable to accept their invitation at this time. Although this was true, having incurred the displeasure of high command he felt it wise to keep well away from Zeiss and Schott. It transpired that this was a prudent move, for the following year Zeiss sued the US government for misappropriating $4,200,000 worth of technical data, laboratory equipment, and manufacturing machinery.

The trainload of Zeiss equipment dispatched by Hub in June 1945 had wound up at Hanau as intended, only to become trapped in the administrative chaos that arose at this time through a succession of personnel assignments and redeployments. Someone decided to send off part of the shipment to Wright Field, USA, and this included much that it was intended to hand over to the Zeiss evacuees who had assembled at Heidenheim. Zeiss made numerous representations to try and retrieve this material, which in the meantime had been mislaid in some army warehouse in the States. The company was next advised to enter into litigation against the US government. Hub, who had by then moved on to a staff job in the Landsberg fighter operations headquarters, received a summons to US Army Headquarters at Heidelberg. They had been asked to interview him to ascertain if he had actually authorized and shipped the lengthy list of items for which the Zeiss people were claiming. Hub's answer was in the affirmative; he confirmed signing the shipping manifests. After protracted litigation Zeiss won their case. Hub felt the affair was a blight on his service career; in future there would be those given to associating his name with the hefty bill paid by the US government. To some degree this was so, although Hub's only crime was to use his initiative in a situation where he had been encouraged to do so.

When, in June 1950, North Korean troops invaded the South, the USA became involved in the hostilities as the major air contingent of the United Nations Force called into action. The new Russian swept-wing jet fighter, the MiG-15, appeared above the battle front and was countered by the F-86 Sabre, the similar American development. Many Second World War aces entered into the action, including some of Hub's former stars in the 56th Fighter Group. Francis Gabreski added six and a half victories to his record and Walker Mahurin was credited with three and a half MiGs before being shot down and made prisoner. While this was going on Hub, in his view, was on the wrong side of the world.

He remained in Germany until the summer of 1954, after which 12 months were spent studying at the Air War College at Maxwell Air Force Base, Montgomery, Alabama, to equip him for a two-year assignment to the Operational Planning Division of the USAF in the Pentagon. This assignment was chiefly concerned with developing operational plans for two advanced jet fighters (F-101 and F-104). It was an arduous and exasperating task, requiring no less than three presentations before receiving final approval from the USAF Air Council.

In August 1955 Hub was again able to escape from a staff desk. He joined Strategic Air Command's force of long-range fighters, commanding the 31st Fighter Wing at Turner Air Force Base, Albany, Georgia, before moving to the controlling 40th Air Division on the same base. The Republic F-84F Thunderstreaks in the division were suffering numerous engine problems. On a cross-country flight the engine of Hub's jet failed, forcing him to eject and float down into a forested area to suffer a broken back. In typical mood, the CO of the Turner fighters took authority to task over the shortcomings of this aircraft hampering the proficiency of his outfit.

Finally, SAC decided long-range fighter support of its current mission was no longer useful, and in the mid-1950s all its fighter units were phased out. The new age of guided missiles and advanced radar tracking systems influenced a policy in which the fast jet bombers of the day would attempt to penetrate an enemy's defenses individually, relying on speed, diversification, and electronic countermeasures to succeed. Senior SAC fighter personnel had an opportunity to stay with the Command. Hub was one who chose to do this, provided he did not become involved in bomber operations.

While at Albany the sad news was received of the death of his pal David Schilling, one of the brightest stars of the 56th Fighter Group's wartime days. Schilling was one of many flamboyant fighter leaders who found it difficult to come to terms with the strictures of the new USAF, and there had also been tragic circumstances in his personal life. Even so, there was no mellowing of his charisma or his taste for high living. A staff assignment in England found him enjoying the social whirl. After one outing, while speeding along in his powerful Allard sports car, he clipped a concrete bridge post with fatal consequences. Though saddened, Hub felt that it was the kind of exit from this life expected of such a personable and exuberant character; Dave was not the sort of man to die in his bed.

In April 1957 Hub took command of the 4080th Strategic Reconnaissance Wing at Laughlin Air Force Base near Del Rio, Texas. The unit operated the new high-flying Lockheed U-2 and Martin B-57E Canberra "spy planes" on "Cuba watching" flights, although this aspect of its operations was secret at the time. Some attitudes and policies of other SAC commanders, reared in the bomber environment, did not find favor with the former fighter colonel and led to some frank exchanges. In particular, Hub had never been afraid to express his disapproval to men of higher rank in wartime, but such plain speaking could be imprudent in the peacetime service if promotion was a goal. Within a few months Hub had reached the decision that a career in SAC was a mistake. So had SAC headquarters. At the end of that year he was given an assignment in the headquarters of the North American Air Defense Command (NORAD) at Colorado Springs.

There were a few fighter men who did adapt quite successfully to the bomber regime in Strategic Air Command. Most notably Gerald Johnson, the 56th's first ace and fellow inmate of Hub's in Stalag Luft I. The genial "Gerry" Johnson eventually rose to the rank of lieutenant general and to command the 8th Air Force in its operations over North Vietnam before retirement in the 1970s. For the Second World War majority who had taken to the sky as the lone captains of their combat aircraft, it remained a case of once a fighter pilot always a fighter pilot. When they could, these men chose to go to Tactical Air Command, based largely upon the fighter-bomber concept where the units retained that distinctive mark of their trade. Indeed, the rule that a fighter cockpit demanded the fast reactions of the young had some exceptions; experience and acquired skill were more important. With the aid of electronic detection and guidance systems, the supersonic jets were as ably handled by 40-year-olds as by those half their age. In the Vietnam conflict one of the most successful aces was "young Robin Olds" of Hub's Wattisham days who, as a colonel turned 43, was responsible for shooting down four MiGs. Having a soft spot for his old Mustang group CO, Olds called his command in Vietnam "The Wolfpack."

For the remainder of his time in the USAF Hub was committed to the inevitable staff appointments that are the lot of an old hand pressing fifty. Nevertheless, he maintained his flying status, although opportunity now only presented liaison and trainer types of aircraft. From NORAD he returned to Europe, this time to Madrid, Spain, where his duties were largely concerned with programming and monitoring the use of some 500 American military aircraft provided for the Spanish forces. His final assignment was as commander of the Reno Air Defense Sector, an organization that oversaw and controlled the defensive fighter and radar installations of five western states. Three and a half years at Reno brought retirement: Hub was 52, and 30 of those years had been spent in the service, 23 as a temporary or full colonel.

An officer of his obvious capabilities and distinction would have been expected to advance to the rank of general, and certainly Hubert Zemke was well qualified to become a general officer. The reason why he did not is to be found in the character of the man.

If Hub believed things had to be said for the good of his command they were said. True to his beliefs to the point of stubbornness, disinclined to turn a blind eye or remain mute if someone exhibited incompetence, he rarely hesitated to admonish or expostulate, even if the transgressor or antagonist was of senior rank. Personal integrity is a fine thing, but the facts of life are that to contest the actions or directives of superiors rarely makes them friends. In such circumstances, when general officer promotion depends on the recommendations of those senior to the candidate, the outcome tends to be a sideways move, not vertical. A more ambitious officer might have held his tongue if folly was evident, something that was not in Hub's nature. To better one's standing in the higher echelons of the service, one could either join the opposition or rise above them to form one's own following. Hub did neither. He became a loner.

A half century on from the Second World War Hubert Zemke is recorded primarily as the most successful and enterprising of United States fighter commanders of that conflict. Yet his subsequent adventures in the land of his forefathers, in particular his presence at Barth and Jena, are further examples of the winning initiative that was his mark.

The Allied prisoner organization at Stalag Luft I was already well organized when Hub arrived. Even so, his representation for 9,000 POWs and handling of the German administration in the days before liberation were most commendable.

As for his plans and impromptu actions at Jena, however much these offended the Soviets and marred his own military career, both Zeiss and Schott have prospered exceedingly in the west. Zeiss remains West Germany's leader in optical devices, with an international reputation and manufacturing facilities in Singapore and the USA in addition to the home plant at Oberkochen. The television camera lenses that covered man's first steps on the moon were made by Zeiss. Schott's progress is equally impressive. Reestablishing production at Mainz in 1951, the 43 evacuees from Jena grew to a worldwide force of 31,000 in an organization that is the acknowledged leader in specialist glass. While this success is of their own making, both famous companies owe more than a little to an erstwhile enemy who only ever wanted to be a fighter pilot.

Index